Successful American Families

OTHER BOOKS BY THESE AUTHORS

BY CARLE C. ZIMMERMAN & LUCIUS F. CERVANTES
Marriage and the Family (1956)

BY CARLE C. ZIMMERMAN
Siam, Rural Economic Survey (1931)
Family and Society (1935)
Studies in Consumption and Standards of Living (1936)
The Changing Community (1939)
Family and Civilization (1947)
Family of Tomorrow (1949)

BY LUCIUS F. CERVANTES
That You May Live (1945)
And God Made Man and Woman (1959)

SUCCESSFUL

AMERICAN

FAMILIES

BY

Carle C. Zimmerman, Ph.D.
Harvard University

and

Lucius F. Cervantes, S.J., Ph.D.
St. Louis University
Ford Foundation Fellow, Harvard University

PAGEANT PRESS, INC.   NEW YORK

PUBLISHED BY PAGEANT PRESS, INC.
101 FIFTH AVENUE, NEW YORK 3, NEW YORK
FIRST EDITION

LIBRARY OF CONGRESS CATALOGUE CARD NUMBER: 60-13116

MANUFACTURED IN THE UNITED STATES OF AMERICA

Dedicated . . .

To the Harvard Laboratory of Social Relations and The Ford Foundation that financed this project, and to the 54,233 families, 9,253 students and 232 school officials who made this study possible.

CONTENTS

LIST OF TABLES

3

4

5

A STUDY OF SUCCESSFUL FAMILIES

chapter I   THIS BOOK IS BASED ON A STUDY OF ABOUT SIXTY
thousand successful American families. These families
either had a child in the senior class of high school, or were the
intimate friends of the child's parents. As of 1955, the families
lived in eight cities of three types—old: Boston, New Orleans
and St. Louis; new: Denver, Omaha and Los Angeles (Long
Beach section), and smaller, semi-rural: Morgantown, West Virginia and Stillwater, Oklahoma. About ten thousand families had
a child in high school; the remaining fifty thousand were best-
friend families.

FAMILY FRIENDS AND SUCCESS

The aim of the study was to evaluate the kind of friends the
student families had, and the significance of family friends upon
"social creativity." In addition, we sought to determine what
influence family friends had on divorce and desertion, juvenile
arrest and the ability of families to keep children in school beyond
the normal compulsory age of sixteen.

Basic factors guiding the course of our work were these:
(1) the avoidance of family disruption by divorce or desertion,
(2) the avoidance of interference by the police and (3) keeping
the children in school. The most "successful" families meet all
three of the tests. Families meeting a lesser number—say two—
we considered "good" families. Families in which the child drops
out of school as soon as it is legally possible for him to take a
job we call "ordinary." Below them is a final category in which
the children quit school without jobs or serious intent to get them.
Here the males drift until summoned for military service, while
the females wait for "something to happen." This is the "poor"
group, the one claimed to be the chief source of juvenile delinquency.[1]

---

[1] See *Education and Juvenile Delinquency,* Senate, Interim Report, 84th
Congress, Washington, D. C., p. 13 *et passim.*

Our study highlights the "successful" and "good" families, not the "ordinary" or "poor." A later survey will correlate findings on "poor" families. However, our present findings on the use that "successful" and "good" families make of their friends as psychological aides explain, in considerable part, the failures of the "ordinary" and "poor" families.

Our justification for the evaluative terms "successful," "good," "ordinary" and "poor" is that we consider education, in a special sense, to be socially creative. We are seeking to evaluate families on their responsiveness to the general American and world situation, and one indication is a willingness to seek increased education.

All the families in our study are either "successful" or "good," and, in general, we shall not attempt to distinguish between them. Both appear to have used a form of family control—namely, their friends—more effectively than "ordinary" or "poor" families. They appear to have a greater responsiveness to cultural "ideals," and the nature of their family-friend groupings has helped them achieve these ideals.

THE PROBLEM OF BROKEN FAMILIES

Any period of transition, such as that we are now going through, has confused cultural values. The confusion is manifest in the family institution by what may be called "polarization," or cleavage to the right and left. This is happening in the United States today. While we have more broken families, we also have more integrated families. (A broken family is one in which the husband-wife relationship is disrupted by death, desertion or quasi-desertion. Quasi-desertion is the avoidance of support payments to spouses and children; a third or more of all aid to dependent mothers and children in the United States is now due to quasi-desertion.)

Although we lack adequate statistics, the number of children who are "half-orphans" must be very large. They are the victims of homes in which there is adult male and female, but which are nevertheless broken. The child lives with a mother or father to whom he is not related by blood; he lives with a step-parent. The influence of quasi-orphanship on child motivation will be noted in detail later on.[2]

THE CITIES CHOSEN

This study seeks to find out, among other things, how families are able to control the value systems of their teen-agers and to send them out into the world with character fixations adequate to meet the challenge of our technical society. To do this, we picked families of high school seniors in six large municipal centers and two smaller ones, which are representative of our national culture: the Pacific, the Arid West, the Wheat Belt, the Corn Belt, the South and the Urban Northeast.

Our study of two semi-rural towns—was supplementary to the city analysis. Since we found the same result as in the cities, Stillwater and Morgantown are not generally included in our tables. In large degree, American family problems have become national, not just rural-urban, or even regional. While they may be accentuated in some areas, the differences are of degree and not of kind. The main battles of our civilization, as far as family morale is concerned, will have to be settled on an urbanized industrial basis, because even rural districts have come to be dominated by urban values.

SUCCESSFUL FAMILIES KEEP CHILDREN IN SCHOOL

In our selected cities, and others like them, families face great

---

[2] Of 54,925,000 persons under 18 years of age in the United States in 1955 about 47,721,000 or 88% had both "parents" present. The others were divided as follows: 602,000 lived with a father only; 5,177,000, a mother only; 970,000, other relatives, and 455,000, non-related persons. The term "parent," however, includes fathers and mothers with adopted children. As of 1955, approximately 10,000 males and 232,000 females under 18 were already married, and 5,000 other females were divorced. It will be seen that the largest group of children not living with both parents were those living with a mother who had not remarried after the death or divorce of her husband (5,177,000). The number living with a mother and stepfather is unknown.

conflicts of values.[3] A central problem is how to keep their children in the educational system.[4]

Educated youths are necessary to our modern technical civilization, both those who graduate from high school and still more those who go on through colleges and professional schools. Each youth and his family faces a dilemma at the youth's sixteenth year, part of which is that in the present confusion of the class system the blue-collared youth can quickly claim high economic rewards, higher even than the youth of the white-collared class. A youngster can choose between the classroom and a good job.[5] The conflict in blue-collared homes has been a fundamental one. At the time of this study and for a decade before it, immediate money rewards had been opposed to social values, family ideals and the needs of our civilization.

By and large "civilization-adequate" families manage to get their children through high school. Our interest is the methods of social organization for character control these families use. The social creativeness of having a child graduate from high school is shown by the fact that of every 25 children who entered the first grade in 1940-41 only 16 finished the eighth grade, and only 11 finished high school.

Those families that kept their children in school through the senior class of high school constitute a minority. Families in our study did this under difficult living conditions in the hearts of large American cities. (We assume that most children dropping out of high school before graduation were perfectly capable of going on if motivated properly.)

In the immediate future the problem of keeping children in

---

[3] On this see Fred K. Vigman, *Crisis of our Cities,* Public Affairs Press, Washington, D. C., 1955.

[4] As of 1957, there were three millions, 18-24 years of age, enrolled in our colleges. These had come from our high school classes of 1952-56. By 1957, this college enrollment will be nearer ten millions. See *Metropolitan Statistical Bulletin,* August, 1959.

[5] The elevation of the "blue collars" above the "white collars" may be only temporary. Post-Sputnik events seem to have changed opinion in the United States about the literate or "egghead" class.

school will become more acute and involve many more millions of families. By 1960 the children born in the period 1945-1950 will be entering high school. They are more numerous by millions than those born in 1938-40 (those we have studied), and more of them will be of the broken-home and quasi-orphan group because of the divorce, desertion, quasi-desertion and other conditions arising from World War II.

THE HYPOTHESIS THAT GOOD FAMILIES ASSOCIATE WITH LIKE FAMILIES

In making our study, our procedure was this: On an appointed day and in lieu of a class period, each senior was asked to fill out a questionnaire on 16 traits of his own family, and 18 of his parental best-friend families—that is, intimate, visiting friends of his parents. The questions were very simple, and we found almost unanimously that the seniors knew the answers and were willing to give them.

Our main hypothesis was that the student's families would surround themselves with other families having similar values. By doing this, the families would create such a home environment that the children would grow up without knowing or hearing very much about conflicting mores and differing values. The children's values would have an opportunity to take root and grow. We believed this similarity of values between families could be measured by similarities in religion, economic status, "region" of origin and intermarriage or kindred relations.

The hypothesis was derived originally from several sources. Historically, our family system has surrounded itself with kindred and "clients." A client, in the classic sense, is a non-kindred who has accepted the obligations of kindred. Families surrounded themselves by kindred and clients to protect themselves against outsiders in those periods of Western society in which there was no strong public system of law and order. Secondly, it is now clearly proved that when men and women marry assortatively (with similar backgrounds and values), they are most successful in family life, as judged by the number of children, infrequency of divorce and desertion and infrequency of juvenile trouble.[6]

We reasoned that civilization-adequate families in our modern American cities might be achieving their aims in the control of the minds of their teen-agers by surrounding themselves with similar families having like ideals and values. Out of this fabric would be created a common socio-psychological image of life, so that everywhere the child looked he would see the same "pictures" he saw in his home. Our ancient families banded together for physical protection. Do our moderns do this for social and mental protection?

Finally, studies of friendship, beginning with that of Aristotle in his *Nichomachean Ethics,* down to Peter Kropotkin's *Mutual Aid* (1902), have shown that friendship has a very significant relation to human society, particularly in times of instability and crisis. When grave threats disturb persons, they fly immediately to kindred and friends for comfort and support.

THE NEW FAMILY TYPE FOR THE SPACE AGE

This study was entered into against background facts of signal importance. The first is that we have entered a new age in which the world has become physically one, whether for good or evil. Every culture is now seeking its freedom and place in the sun.[7] Second, the new age demands a stronger, more resolute and better equipped individual. Third, to produce such persons will demand a reorganization of the present family system and the building of one that is stronger educationally and morally. And, finally, the family system is in a generally weakened state from the rapid urbanization of the past century, which makes reorganization difficult. Our generation has to meet many new and old problems on a grand scale.

Early in January, 1957, Russia exploded an atomic bomb, and

---

[6] See Zimmerman-Cervantes, *Marriage and the Family,* Regnery, Chicago, 1956, p. 609, for documentation of this similarity in marriage.

[7] See the foreword to P. A. Sorokin, *Social and Cultural Dynamics,* Vol. I, American Book Co., New York, 1937, where the present rise of "new" cultures all over the world is discussed.

American scientists monitored its fallout of fission products. Non-stop simulated bomber flights in the upper atmosphere were now reported by the United States as traveling around the world in about forty-five hours. Trouble arose in the Middle East. Hungary broke into revolution. Then came Sputnik, space vehicles, ICBM's and crash programs for training more scientists. The world is like a volcano that breaks out repeatedly.

THE FAMILY SYSTEM IS CHANGING EVERYWHERE

The world approaches this critical period with a grave disruption of the family system. Family disintegration, which was once claimed by Europe to be almost entirely "American corruption," now circles the globe, and, in some areas, is still increasing. It makes no difference whether we take up the situation in the continent of Africa, in Eastern or Western Europe, in Asia or in the Americas, North and South, the family crisis is found as epidemic.

Previous disruptions of a family system have been largely localized, as among the peoples in the Roman Empire in the early centuries of our Christian era, or among the Arabic peoples in the century that saw the birth and rise of Mohammedanism. But in the modern world little is or can be kept localized. Consequently, while this is a study of the United States, it has implications that are world-wide.[8]

---

[8] The world-wide disruption of the family system, due in part to changes in family values and in part to cultural changes, is documented in the following works: Carle C. Zimmerman, *Family and Civilization*, Harper & Bros., New York, 1947; Carle C. Zimmerman and L. F. Cervantes, S. J., *Marriage and the Family*, Henry Regnery Co., Chicago, 1956; Anna Freud and Dorothy T. Burlingham, *War and Children* and *Infants Without Families*, International Press, New York, 1943; Eliot Slater and Moya Woodside, *Patterns of Marriage*, Cassel and Co., London, 1951; Colloques Internationaux de la Recherche Scientifique, *Sociologie Comparée de la Famille Contemporaine*, Editions du Centre National de la Recherche Scientifique, Paris, 1955; R. Schlesinger, *Changing Attitudes in Soviet Russia: The Family*, Routledge and Kegan Paul, London, 1949; Arthur Phillips (Ed.) *Survey of African Marriage and Family Life*, Ox-

BASIC FINDINGS CONCERN FRIENDSHIP RELATIONS
WITH KINDRED AND LIKE FAMILIES

Before we embark on a detailed account, a brief resume of
some of our basic findings may be helpful. Our statistics show
that successful American families allow into their homes and
circles of intimacy only other families remarkably like themselves. This is shown, first of all, by the *proportion of kindred*
among the friend-families. Secondly, it is clear that the *friend-
families are of the same backgrounds* as the parent families. This
is evident in similarities of regions of origin. Third, the *friends
are pronouncedly of the same religious, moral and ethical views*
as the parents. This is measured by the similarities of religious
confessions. Fourth, *parents generally select friends of similar
tastes* as measured roughly by income groups.

The successful families acquired very similar friends soon
after marriage and continued close, intimate, visiting relations
with them over many years. If new acquaintances failed to measure
up to the ideals of the parental family, they were soon avoided
and dropped. They were replaced by others who *did* fit the
family's needs. As a result, the children of the families tended
to know most intimately only adults (the parents of the friend-
families) who were remarkably like their own parents in values,
backgrounds and outlook on life.

Thus the parents had created little separate "domestic
worlds," something like solar systems in a larger universe. These
social sub-systems around the home were clearly distinct and
different from the wider worlds of strangers, and of "ordinary"
and "poor" families. We think the children of such homes seem

---

ford University Press, New York, 1953; The Association of American Law
Schools, *Essays on Family Law,* Foundation Press, Brooklyn, 1950; J. L.
Thomas, S. J., *The American Catholic Family,* Prentice-Hall, Englewood
Cliffs, New Jersey, 1956; P. A. Sorokin, *The American Sex Revolution,*
Porter Sargent, Boston, 1956; E. Franklin Frazier, *The Negro Family in
the United States* (2nd ed.), University of Chicago Press, Chicago, 1957.
In the Asiatic countries, Australia and South America, disruption for the
same or different reasons is actual or beginning.

to feel a sort of protection, and "difference," from the other world, much as persons in the cabin of an airliner feel separate from the world of rarified air and cold space just beyond the walls and windows.

SIMILAR FAMILY-FRIENDS PROTECT THE GOOD VALUES

However, this protection and isolation within the family-friendship system is not physical, but social. It is a type of natural social psychiatry. It consists of a surrounding of values and beliefs, measurable but intangible. It is made up of layers of friend-families, with each layer consisting not merely of the friend-family itself, but *its* friends as well. Nearly always, the friend-family has regularly visited within the parent-family home since the child was an infant, and first began to realize there were other persons in the world than its mother. Soon after the child had been able to identify its father, brothers and sisters, it had become conscious of the family friends.

These layers of family friends were by no means identical. Those who composed the first "social layer" (and were generally seen about the home most often during the most years) were most like the child's family. The first layer was more like the child's parents than the second, the second than the third, the third than the fourth and so on through all the persons the child regularly saw about the home.

Because of these surrounding layers, the child slowly and unconsciously began to differentiate between two worlds—his home-oriented one, which he thought the "right" one, and to be trusted and emulated—and another, the stranger-oriented, which was neither to be trusted nor emulated. The gap between these two worlds was marked off for him by the outermost circle of friend families. In a sense, the friend families also provided him, as he grew up, with a bridge to the outer world through their own friend-families, who were not necessarily friends of his parents, although usually not markedly different from them in values.

FRIEND VALUE SYSTEMS DIRECT CHILD MOTIVATION

In this type of situation, the child apparently tends to accumulate a deep-grained, fundamental, unconscious sympathy with basic values similar to his parents', and where these are "good," or culturally-oriented, such as towards avoidance of divorce, delinquency and low academic competency, he tends to become "civilization-adequate."

However, this is not all. The relation between the parent-family and the friend-families is not one-way, but a mutual and retroactive one. As the friend-families show a remarkable ability to strengthen the parent-family, so the parent-family tends to strengthen the friend-families. It is a mutual causal-functional influence.

The more parents are able to select and have about them friends with the same ideals and values the more are the children disposed to be creative, e.g., to proceed further in the educational process. And the more the child has a good relationship with his parents, the stronger becomes his family, and the stronger the friend-families. This will be shown in detail for all groups in all cities as we proceed with this study.

Thus, without going into sociological jargon, it can be said that much social creativity (probably as much as lies within the limits of capability) is achieved by implanting adult ideals in children through forming intimate, similar friend-family groups. These help the parent ideals develop and be accepted by the children. It is a combination of a will or desire on the parents' part to achieve higher goals, and the proper group implantation of the will or desire in the children.

"PROTECTED VALUE SYSTEMS" ARE A "NEW" INVENTION

We wish to emphasize that the creation and use of friendship groupings by parent families in urban environments is a "new" social invention. One or two generations ago, nearly all these families lived "somewhere else," in peasant villages of Europe or other rural communities. The mass settling and urbanization of these people in the cities of America between 1850 and 1910 broke up all former social relations.

Most of the parents we studied were born in the United States between 1905 and 1915, but did not at the time of our survey (1952-55) live in the communities of their birth. What social organization they had at the time of our survey was one they themselves had formed from new neighbors in a new environment. While the principle of family friendships is as old as mankind, the knowledge and use of this principle by these people in the environment in which they live is their own invention.

Our study shows that out of the present social situation has come a capacity for the onward march of the American people into the new technical world of the Atomic Age. In the final two chapters of this study on *Successful American Families* we shall integrate the more restricted statistical and empirical conclusions of this study with broader sociological theory and social history. Without discussing our over-all plan and general results further, we now wish to take up certain aspects of the troubled modern family system and explain why a new type of family-friendship grouping of fundamental social importance has appeared.

THE PEOPLE STUDIED

chapter II THIS STUDY OF THE PRESENT AMERICAN FAMILY
system started with the problem of how families
control the motivation of teen-agers and particularly how they get
them to finish high school. The striving for greater educational
accomplishment is a basic and socially desirable process in modern
life. Life is a sort of one-way, one-chance, no second-choice
process. Youthful decisions generally dominate the whole after-
pattern of life. To continue in school or to drop out is a key
decision of the teen-ager.

In order to find out the influential circumstances of this decision we studied the family friendships of their parents. These
friendships can be considered a distinctly important psychiatric
device used by parents in the control of child motivation. To test
our hypothesis, some thousands of high school seniors were
asked to fill out questionnaires about their families and the
friends of their families.

HOW THE STUDY WAS MADE

Each high school senior was asked to list his parents' intimate
friends, and arrange them in order of nearness or closeness to
his parents. He was requested to answer eighteen questions about
them. He was told to list at least five family friends, if his parents
had that many, and to enumerate more if he felt these additional
friends particularly important. This method has been developed
over a period of years in the family research projects at Harvard
University and similar studies have been made many times with
different groups.

Other studies have shown that most parents have only five
or six really intimate friends. We found in the high schools that
five friend-families were generally the important ones in the mind
of the child. Personal interviews with students further confirmed

the figure of five or six. Beyond five or six friend-families, persons became more-or-less casual visitors, not permitted to penetrate very deeply into the family's intimate affairs. Of course, through knowing friends of the friend-families, children do learn something about additional "similar people," but not in great detail.

The present study was made with the aid of city school superintendents, high school principals and teachers. On a given day in a class which all had to take, high school seniors were told about the study and asked to fill out the questionnaires as the exercise for that day. The sheets were picked up at the end of the exercise, and no time was permitted for discussion, misinterpretation or for jocularity. The students were not permitted to take the blanks home.

If a student finished his questionnaire before his classmates, he was asked to turn it over and write on the back an essay on "a good family." This was to keep him busy and to prevent reflection upon the need for editorializing his answers. Except for students who were sick or absent for other reasons, returns were approximately a hundred per cent. In only a half dozen cases at the most was the questionnaire taken lightly, and such questionnaires were rejected.

THE INFORMATION CONCERNS PARENTS AND
PARENTAL FRIENDS

The study was made with the full cooperation of superintendents, principals and teachers. They showed a determination to do it right, to permit a minimum of errors, and to get the study over with at one class session. The students knew the answers to most of the questions. Since the average senior had lived in his family for eighteen years the things he was asked to tell about it and its friends were part of his intimate knowledge. From three-fifths to two-thirds of the family friends he reported on had been known to him for more than ten years in the surroundings of his home. The answers showed that the student knew the commonplace details of his family's friends almost as well as of his own. Table I gives the cities, the classes, the number of seniors, the numbers of their family friends studied.

Table 1

THE FAMILIES OF THE STUDY BY CITY*

City	Senior class year	Number of seniors' families	Number of Family-friend families	Selection principles
Boston	54-55	1217	6085	Four parochial and four matched public high schools
New Orleans	54-55	954	4770	All parochial high schools (no public)
Denver	54-55	1250	6250	All high schools
Omaha	54-55	1433	7163	All high schools
St. Louis	54-55	2526	12630	All high schools
Los Angeles	52-53 and 55	1873	8082	All high schools of the Long Beach part
Total		9253	44980	

* We do not present here the data on the two rural towns, Stillwater, Oklahoma, and Morgantown, West Virginia. These results were omitted both for simplicity's sake and because they merely corroborated our general findings.

The study is a specific type of sampling of the complete universe of the "metropolitan areas" of these cities. It was started first in a section of greater Los Angeles, the port city of Long Beach, in 1952-53. At that time it did not include the parochial schools, but these, with a graduating class of 241, were added in 1955. In New Orleans we were unable to get to the public schools because of the turmoil engendered by school integration.

The city studied last was Boston. Here we decided that 1200 questionnaires were sufficient; we took four parochial high schools and matched them with four public high schools covering the same areas. Of the resulting eight schools, two were upper-middle class, four middle class and two in poor areas. The eight schools involved 7302 families.

ALL RACES AND ETHNIC GROUPS INCLUDED

No questions were asked about the race, color or ethnic origin of the students. However, in St. Louis the study was made the year before the integration of the schools, and we know that 290 seniors in Negro schools gave us answers involving about 1500 Negro families of that city. Also one of the parochial schools in New Orleans, with about 100 seniors, gave us results relating to about 600 Negro families of that city. This totals more than 2,000 Negro families identified as such.

"Color" or "race" as a factor in friendship was not studied the same way as such influences as religion, region of origin, kinship or economic standing. Thus, when we refer to family behavior in St. Louis or New Orleans, we refer to white and Negro alike, since these cities are composed of white and Negro persons. In the same way, when we analyze Los Angeles or Denver, we include the families of Mexican, Spanish, or Spanish-American origin, as well as Negroes. All are Americans and have generally followed the same principles of social organization.

THE STUDY CONCERNS "GOOD" FAMILIES ONLY

Before we go further into the characteristics of the families studied, it may be helpful if we point out some of the things which can and cannot be established from the data secured. Since this is not a study of the "average" American family, the tables cannot be used to make "national averages." We are not interested in national averages as such. What we wish to find out is how the "better" or more successful families conduct themselves.

Neither is this a study of the best families in America, nor a mathematically exact sample of the best families. The sample includes "all" the better families in the municipal districts of

six big, regionally representative cities that had a child in the
senior high school class of the selected year, or were close
friends of those families. Where we do not have "all" families—
as in Boston, New Orleans and Los Angeles—we have all of a
type sample, as all of eight representative high schools of Boston,
all of the port city Long Beach (nearly 300,000 population),
a part of greater Los Angeles, or all of the parochial schools of
New Orleans. In no case did we include suburban families, unless
the children from these were in a parochial or public high
school of the central city.

From 10 to 16 per cent of the families studied had incomes
of more than $10,000 a year. No more than 5 to 14 per cent had
incomes of less than $2000 a year. If Boston has a high per-
centage of foreign born, certainly this is not true for New Orleans
nor the mid-Western cities. If Boston is highly Catholic, others
are highly Protestant. Others have a large percentage of the
newer sects, called here generally the "Pentecostalites," and Long
Beach has a large number of Mormons.[1]

Averages and medians have little meaning for our study be-

---

[1] Pentecostalite is used to denote a number of new branches or sects
within Christianity which have flowered during the twentieth century. Historically, Protestantism was a term applied to any sect of the Christian
Churches which was not old Catholic, Roman Catholic, or Eastern (Greek
Orthodox) Catholic, although the designation was repudiated by some of
them—for example, the Anglicans. The term became more inclusive with
time. In the seventeenth century the main Protestant bodies were the
Lutherans and Anglicans; in the eighteenth century new churches were
accepted in common thinking as "Protestant," such as Methodists and
Baptists. In the nineteenth century still other sects proliferated, many of
them designating themselves by adjectives preceding the Church name, a
"Primitive Baptists" (1835), "Free Methodists" (1860) or "Cumberland
Presbyterians" (1810). The Pentecostalite Churches (so-called here because of the definition, "religious excitement accompanied by ecstatic
utterances, interpreted as the gift of tongues, as at Pentecost") have not
yet generally accepted the designation "Protestant." These churches are
growing rapidly in number and membership, both in the "key-towns" of
the Cornbelt and the Wheatbelt in interior America, and in the central
districts of the metropolitan areas located there. The word is used only
in a descriptive sense.

.use, in a technical sense, this is not a study of typical America, ral-urban, city-suburban or otherwise. On the other hand, it typical in that it takes a regional approach to the basic social ·ocess of psychiatric control of family motivation for at least ·κ of the seven great American regions. We have taken the families which have demonstrated their success by getting their aildren into the senior class of high schools under the most fficult circumstances and we have delved deeply into a key, if ·ɔt *the* key process in the development and enrichment of com- g American culture. Our study is of an "ideal type," or of a ·ɔup most conspicuous in achieving a fundamental goal against eat odds.

ᴇMBERSHIP IN RELIGIOUS GROUPS

One of the fundamentals in family organization and prac- ·ce is, of course, religion. We need not go into the long history religious doctrine and the religious control of family law ɾough many centuries. Suffice it to say that even with today's ·velopment of secular law, religious groups still have their own formal doctrines about family behavior. Table 2 summarizes ·e religious creeds of the mothers of the high school seniors for ·e cities studied, except for Los Angeles. There the father's ligion alone was taken because of the high importance of

Table 2

RELIGION OF MOTHERS OF SENIORS
Percentages

·ty	Protestant	Catholic	Jewish	Other	None
·ston	11	80	6	2	*
·w Orleans	5	92	—	1	1
Louis	27	56	4	11	2
·nver	43	47	2	6	2
·naha	39	48	3	8	2
·s Angeles†	58	12	3	16	11

Less than one per cent.
Based upon father's religion due to the Mormon influence.

Mormonism in the city and on the advice of members of tha
faith.

While Table 2 pertains to mothers of the 9,253 high schoc
senior families reported upon, it is identical with one for thei
friends, and applies to all families. (Because of this virtua
identity we do not present the friend-family distribution.) Ther
were, however, minor exceptions among the Catholics and th
so-called "no-religion group" in Los Angeles. Seniors' father
revealed 12 per cent Catholics; "all friends," 15 per cent; father
were 11 per cent "nones"; "all friends," 8 per cent. We show
later that persons claiming "no religion" are an extreme grou]
which tends to revert in part toward some type of religiou
adherence and in doing so gain in family life.

Our survey revealed a notable intermixing of faiths, particu
larly through cross-marriages.

RELIGIOUS GROUPS VARY BY CITY

The most Catholic city in our study is Boston and the mos
Protestant is Los Angeles. In Boston, where Catholics are
majority of the population, even the public schools have a pre
dominance of that faith. Los Angeles would be even mor
Protestant except that Mormons do not ordinarily call them
selves "Protestants," no matter what others may call them
Protestants and "others" in Los Angeles are three-quarters o
the people studied.

New Orleans appears to have an unduly high percentage o
Catholics in the sample but it must be remembered that th
study there was of parochial schools only.[2]

---

[2] Catholicism in New Orleans and Southern Louisiana arose as a sor
of historical accident. The state was a fashionable French Crow:
colony after 1731. It was ceded to Spain in 1763 and returned to Franc
in 1801 after which, in 1803, it came to the United States as part of th
Louisiana Purchase. Between 1760 and 1790 about 4,000 Acadians, o
French-Canadians, expelled by the British from Nova Scotia came to th
area and their descendants are called "Cajuns" today. Then after th
French Revolution of 1789 a large number of French Royalists, fleein
from the Terror, migrated there.

Table 2 mirrors the striking fact that Catholics are predominantly urban—the exceptions being small groups in Wisconsin, Louisiana and among the Spanish-Americans of the Southwest. Our careful sampling gave an unexpectedly high incidence of Catholics. In St. Louis, an area surrounded by Protestants, the municipal high school students and their friends were 56 per cent Catholic.

GEOGRAPHICAL DISTRIBUTION OF RELIGIOUS GROUPS

A second fact of importance is the regional and geographic distribution of the Protestant and Catholic faiths in the United States. Boston, in a large degree, is the "geographic" center of Catholicism in America. It is one of a dozen cities in the Urban-Northeast (a triangle bounded by lines connecting Chicago, Philadelphia and Boston) which has more than a million persons

---

Much of the Catholicism in the urban northeast region of the United States originated with the migrations of the Irish, beginning after 1840, and the coming of the Italians and French Canadians for industrial work, mostly after 1900. Thus, in New Orleans, the "old settlers" are Catholic whereas in the Urban-Northeast, the "old" ones are mostly Protestant. We point this out as a background for interpretation.

In St. Louis, Catholicism has some of the flavor of the old pre-revolutionary settlement, made in 1764 as a collection point by the French fur traders. At that time the interior of the country was under French domination. The settlement was near the joining place of the Missouri and Mississippi Rivers, which drain much of the interior of the continent east of the Rockies and south of the Great Lakes. But the Catholics gained predominant influence in St. Louis with the great wave of German immigration to America after the first quarter of the nineteenth century. German influence predominated by the time of the American Civil War.

These Catholic Germans were a strong influence (along with the hill people of the Ozarks, who were also against slavery) in finally aligning this former slave state (The Missouri Compromise Act of 1820) with the Northern States during that Civil War. The major addition to Catholicism in St. Louis in this century has been through the immigration of Italians there. Consequently St. Louis is a compromise between the older settled Catholicism of New Orleans and the newer elements in the urban northeast.

of Catholic faith; these cities contain about half of all the Catholics in the United States.

A third important fact is that if one draws three lines across the United States, one starting at Los Angeles, another at Portland, Oregon, and the third at the Gulf Coast in Georgia, all converging on Boston, one end of each line will be among a predominantly Protestant population and the other end in the highly concentrated Urban-Northeast Catholic group.[3]

Jews, as a minority group, are located principally in the North, and on the East Coast, particularly in cities. The Boston sample of families reported 6 per cent Jews. A different selection of schools would have given a higher percentage for Boston because the U.S. census reports a large Jewish population in the city.

New Orleans reported no Jews in the senior classes of the parochial schools and few Jewish friends. The census reports very few Jews in New Orleans. In Denver and Omaha, 2 and 3 per cent reported themselves as Jews as contrasted with 4 per cent in St. Louis. Los Angeles had 3 per cent of Jews in senior class families

---

[3] Despite the divergent regional and ideological patterning of the Protestant and Catholic segments of the American society there has been a largely unrecognized unity which is of capital psychological importance for the collective mentality of the United States. The stronger Protestant groupings and the Catholic are all "fundamentalists" in the sense of being highly "doctrinal" in regard to rules of personal behavior. Even though their isolation from one another has prevented their common awareness of the fact, each group has a "familistic" doctrine. With the growth of religious interests both among the Westward-facing Protestants and the Eastward-facing Catholics there has likewise been a nation-wide growth of family interests. The broadening and strengthening of the fundamentalist religious conviction and its consequent strengthening of the familistic spirit may be a basic reason for the recent upward swing of the American birth rate especially as manifested among the educated classes. No one has yet explained why and how our population processes have changed direction in the families of persons born after 1915 within the United States. We cannot go into a lengthy discussion of the matter here but this change among a free democratic population is, in a fundamental sense, pretty much unique to our time and to our country. Lacking adequate other explanations, this regionalism of "fundamentalists" in a free country may be a basic "cause."

and 4 per cent among their friends. (The Jews of Los Angeles, as analyzed elsewhere, were very prone to associate with one another. By random selection, they would have had only a small percentage of Jewish friends; in actuality, the percentage was thirty times greater.) [4]

PERSONS CLAIMING "NO RELIGION" FOUND MOSTLY IN WESTERN CITIES

Two other comments seem important about the table on religious faith among high school groups. One concerns the concentration of persons claiming "no religion" in Long Beach. The samples of families studied in Boston and Long Beach were about equally numerous (7,302 for Boston and 8,759 Long Beach) but the Boston group reported 24 "nones" or "non-believers" while the Long Beach groups claimed 771.

Then finally, the high proportions of "other religions" in St. Louis, Omaha and Denver, should be commented on. The term, meaning religions other than Protestantism, Catholicism and Judaism, has a different meaning in various cities. In Long Beach "others" seem mostly Mormons. The "others" in the interior of the nation, as we are informed by the school teachers, are primarily "Pentecostalites." In Boston, many of the "others" are Christian Scientists or of the Greek Orthodox Church.

These remarks on religious faiths are merely to introduce the study. A later analysis will deal with the influence of faith and orthodoxy upon family success.

RICH AS WELL AS POOR FAMILIES ARE COVERED

Recruitment through the high schools of a new "creative minority," to use the Toynbeean expression, or the leadership for tomorrow, involves all economic classes. The income groups were divided into four classes: up to $2000; $2000 to $5000;

---

[4] See Carle C. Zimmerman and C. B. Broderick, "Nature and Role of Informal Family Groups," *Marriage and Family Living,* May, 1954, p. 107.

$5000 to $10,000; and above $10,000. The students apparently knew very well the economic standing of their families and their parental-friend families and reported them accordingly.

In some cases, parental mores against discussing any details of wealth, such as those of the Jews and certain groups originating in Northern Italy, made students omit the question on income. However, we know from observation that these people are as wealthy if not more so than the others, so our figures do not overstate the case.

Table 3
ECONOMIC STATUS
OF
HIGH SCHOOL SENIOR FAMILIES
AND THEIR FRIENDS

Percentages by Income Groups

City	up to $2000	$2000 to $5000	$5000 to $10,000	$10,000 or more
Boston				
Students	5	40	44	11
Friends	5	39	43	13
New Orleans				
Students	14	38	34	14
Friends	12	39	34	15
St. Louis				
Students	9	40	38	13
Friends	9	37	38	16
Denver				
Students	8	42	39	11
Friends	10	41	37	12
Omaha				
Students	7	43	39	11
Friends	8	39	38	15
Long Beach				
Students	7	40	43	10
Friends	7	38	41	14

The distribution of income among the seniors' families and their parental friends is given in Table 3.

We report two sets of figures in this table, one for the student families and one for the friend-families. The differences between the two sets deserve comment.

The friend-families appear to be much younger than the parental families. On the average, they have been married a shorter time and have fewer children. This is due in a large part, as will be explained in the next chapter, because *kindred* form an average of two out of five friends. Even in Los Angeles, a city quickly formed by migrants from the middle classes out of the interior of the United States, kindred are three out of every ten family friends.

THE YOUNGER FRIEND-FAMILIES WERE MORE PROSPEROUS

We expected that the younger groups of family friends would have lower incomes than the older groups. However, this was not true. In the poorer groups, under $2000 income, every distribution of family friends was doing better than, or as well as, the parental families, except in Denver and Omaha. In Denver, 8 per cent of the parental families had incomes less than $2000 a year and the friends, 10 per cent. In Omaha the respective figures were 7 per cent for parental families under $2000 and 8 per cent for the friends.

In the best-off groups, with incomes of $10,000 or above, the friends, in all cases, had slightly larger incomes than the parental families. In Boston the figures for $10,000 or more included 11 per cent of the parents, and 13 per cent of the friends. In New Orleans it was 14 as compared with 15 for the friends; in St. Louis, 13 as compared with 16; in Denver 11 as compared with 12; in Omaha, 11 as compared with 15; and in Los Angeles 10, as compared with 14.

The reasons for this are probably several. Incomes are more closely equated with capability than age or seniority, and these friends, though younger, had two advantages. First, they were younger, and hence more active. Second, they belonged to the classes which, by their adherence to the *educational ladder,* indicated they were "ambitious," they not only wanted to, but were, getting "ahead." Finally, the modern tendency, induced by the shortage of educated technical persons, is to pay higher incomes at the start of employment than was the case formerly, and these younger persons had reaped the benefit.

Finally, some tendency exists, natural in such a society as ours, for persons to climb socially. In many respects, of two friends equally liked and fitting to the family, the preference is given to those doing the better economically.

EDUCATED CLASSES BEGINNING TO PROSPER

Several further comments need to be made on income distribution. The persons using the educational ladder come from all economic classes, and most of them are doing well.

Generally, all our statistics show higher incomes for the families studied than the incomes reported for the respective cities in the national census of 1949. This is partly because incomes in the United States rose rapidly between 1949 and 1955. Also our figures are for "family" not "individual," incomes, which the census reports, and our family heads are older than the average "person" of the Census. But they also show the tendency of the educated to rise economically.

Finally, our study confirms and refines the conclusions about "successful" families reached by Paul C. Glick and others of the U.S. Census Bureau, after a careful analysis of income returns for 1946. Glick found that "successful" families, measured merely by the fact the wage earner was living with his first wife after an average of twelve years of marriage, did better economically than those in which the wage earner was living with a subsequent wife. In 1946 the difference was found by Glick to be $300 per family. Our measure of family success is more definitive and exclusive than the index used by Glick.

REGIONAL CITIES IN THE U.S. ARE DIFFERENT

In another work, in which one of the authors collaborated, it was demonstrated that American regions differ in manners, expressions, tastes and points of view.[5] Such differences appear in the present study.

It is our hypothesis that these differences, based on region of origin, partly measure "likenesses" in the selection of family friends. The study used cities, as far as possible, from geographic areas that fairly approximate the great American regions (such as the Urban-Northeast, the Cornbelt, the Wheatbelt, the South, the arid West and the Pacific).

In considering regional differences, it must be kept in mind that American cities are, to considerable degree, composed of the children and grandchildren of migrants. Several principles have dominated migration to cities and these have not been the same for all cities or all periods. Sometimes the preservation or building up of a strong family system has been at cross-purposes with the building up of an urban population. Migration as a youth to a city is one thing. Rearing a family in the city is another. Getting the children through high school is a third.

For certain facets of these intermixed problems, consider Table 4 which contains the percentage distribution by regions of origin for the fathers of the seniors and the fathers of the families of the parental friends. In this summary introductory chapter only a few regional traits will be noted from these distributions.

CITY PEOPLE ARE MOSTLY FROM NEARBY REGIONS

Most of the people in a city come from its surrounding region, if they are not born in the city itself. Where there is a "foreign" body in a city (such as foreign-born in Boston or "midwesterners" in Los Angeles) these "foreigners" attract others because people like to be where there are others of their kind. This is an old principle of migration and need not be discussed further here.

Thus a city like Boston becomes more or less a "closed social system" to other regions in the United States because a

---

[5] See Carle C. Zimmerman and Richard E. DuWors, *Graphic Regional Sociology*, Phillips Book Store, Cambridge, 1953.

Table 4

REGION OF ORIGIN
OF
FAMILIES OF HIGH SCHOOL SENIORS
AND
THEIR FRIEND-FAMILIES

City	Pacific	Rocky Mts.	Mid-West	South-west	South	North-east	Foreign
Boston							
Parents	2	1	1	1	2	66	27
Friends	4	2	3	2	2	69	18
New Orleans							
Parents	*	*	2	2	89	2	5
Friends	1	1	2	3	88	2	3
St. Louis							
Parents	1	1	63	5	16	6	8
Friends	4	2	65	7	12	5	5
Denver							
Parents	2	40	30	4	7	9	8
Friends	9	49	21	4	5	7	5
Omaha							
Parents	1	1	79	1	4	4	10
Friends	3	3	76	4	3	4	7
Los Angeles							
Parents	13	6	37	7	8	21	8
Friends	27	6	29	7	7	17	7

* Less than one per cent.

very high percentage of the "Improper Bostonians" are the Italians, Irish and Jews, or their lately-come relatives and friends from the original homelands overseas. New Orleans is practically a closed social system to other Southerners born "up-state" or "out-state." These are the two cities in which the sample was composed of "more than ninety per cent" of persons either born in the city or, in the case of the foreign-born in Boston of persons who are similar in background and tastes to those born there.

St. Louis is in a medium position. Two-thirds of its high school group are midwesterners, and it is a midwestern city. The remainder represent largely southerners moving north for industrial jobs or foreign-born coming in to be with persons similar to them. In 1950 the St. Louis metropolitan area had forty-two thousand foreign-born whites and a hundred and fifty-four thousand Negroes. The foreign-born there were primarily Germans, Irish and Italians. The Negroes were southerners who, if they went to New Orleans, would find vigorous economic competition with the southern Louisiana Negroes—many of whom are Catholics.

Denver, on the edge of the Midwest, but a mountain state, draws heavily from both Midwest and mountains. Omaha, between the Cornbelt and the Wheatbelt, both ordinarily called "Midwest," gets its predominant population from the surrounding regions. Long Beach, a city assembled out of native Americans during the past half century, has migrants from the Midwest and the Northeast predominating even over those from the Pacific region. That is why it is largely a "Protestant" city: internal migration is mostly a movement of native-born, who in the rural interior are mostly Protestants.

As might be expected, regional minorities in a city tend to have regional friends. In relatively closed social systems like Boston and New Orleans, and largely St. Louis, the small regional minorities choose their friends much more from their region than chance would suggest. Parents of seniors in Boston are only one per cent from the Midwest but their friends are three per cent. Exceptions to this are persons with a social "disability" as "foreign-born" in Boston and "southerners" in the new social climates of St. Louis, Denver, Omaha and Long Beach.

SOCIAL EFFECTS OF GROUPINGS AMONG 54,000 FAMILIES

This descriptive chapter shows the results of comparable data on about 54,000 American families, those with seniors in high school and their immediate friends, living in six large cities. "Chance," or random selection of family friends, would practically eliminate any great similarity of friendship groups by religious confession, ethnic origin, economic standards or regional tastes in these cities. Our tables suggest principles other than random selections. Now that we have set up the problem, we can measure how people get family friends, their likenesses with each other, and the influence of these principles of selection upon family success.

Before we start this analysis, however, we have to study the inner nature of friendship groups. Who compose the friends of these families? How many do they have and how long have they known them? Where do they get their friends? Is the so-called isolated urban family, emphasized by the majority of current sociologists, a fact or a figment of imagination? How many broken families are there among the high school group? How are they broken—by death, by divorce or desertion or by juvenile arrests? These and a number of other questions will now be placed under scrutiny.

THE SOCIAL SYSTEM OF "GOOD" FAMILIES

chapter III   THE PREVIOUS CHAPTERS SUGGEST THAT WE BELIEVE
that too much attention has been paid to the hypo-
thetical "isolated individual," the "man for himself" or that
essentially similar person, the member of "the lonely crowd."
Where the first two types exist, they at least seem to be fringe
phenomena, a few non-typical adults, persons faltering in their
human roles and failing to participate in the social system. Or
perhaps they reflect the psychology of the authors who write these
works more than of the people described.

The ordinary youth who eventually becomes civilization-
adequate lives a long number of adolescent years during which he
is given his "recruit training" in a status role within a family.
Modern society, instead of releasing the individual early from
his "nonage" now tries to keep him in this status role of dependent
learner through high school, through college and through professional school. The days of a Robinson Crusoe, the man meeting the world alone—if such a person ever existed as a major
force in our society—are now over.

FAMILIES ARE NOT PART OF THE LONELY CROWD

The eighteenth century rationalists and the nineteenth century
classical economists claimed that the social contract was brittle.
If it was, it is no longer. John Bunyan (1628-1688) lived about
the same time as Defoe, the author of Robinson Crusoe (1661-
1731). Bunyan wrote the immortal *Pilgrim's Progress* in which
the idea of the lonely individual on his trip through life was given
as the type of new world then coming into being, the society of
today. Christian sought the "straight and narrow way" alone,
without encumbrance of wife, child or old friend.

Whatever may have been the truth of this picture from the
days of Bunyan and Defoe to the end of the classical industrial

system about World War I, the situation it portrays is now clearl
no longer characteristic or possible. The modern person, whethe
a baby in his mother's arms, the high school student with hi
books, or the employee of General Electric or General Motors, is
factually speaking, always a member of a status-group family
and other status and contractual groups derived from, and closel
related to the family.

General Electric was not, of course, organized and set up b
the students' families, but the income and perquisites derived b
an employee from that corporation, after taxes (a status-derive
obligation), go to the family. Family savings come, in large
part, from the compulsory savings, lay-away and social securit
plans. The employee-status is the origin of the paraphernalia c
family life: houses, furnishings, etc., and the family savings ar
largely liquidated for the support of the aged and widowed wh
remain after the death of the husband and father.

Persons today belong to groups, and our study concerns th
transitional groups between the family and the outer world. Hov
universal and frequent are family friends? How numerous ar
they? How long do they last? Do they, in the large cities, includ
kindred? On what bases are they formed? How do people fin
family friends? These questions we seek to answer in this chapter

MOST "GOOD" FAMILIES HAVE FIVE CLOSE-FRIEND UNITS

Table 5 gives the distribution of student families by th
number of their friends. Depending upon the city, from 70 t
86 per cent of all families reported on five or more friend-families
As was said earlier, students were told to report on all ver
intimate family friends.

In Table 5 we find a pattern which will become more fam
iliar as we proceed in this study, namely differences betwee
the older and the newer cities in settled social relations. Th
study shows most friends per family in the older cities, whic
have been most influenced by orthodox religions, and amon
ethnic groups of more recent arrival in the United States. Citie
like Boston and St. Louis have four-fifths of their families report

ing five or more friends. Probably the New Orleans figure is higher (86 per cent) than it would have been if the study had included public, as well as parochial, schools. This, however, is only an opinion; the city is very old and may generally have a high percentage of relatively immobile people.

The families reporting *"no friends,"* constitute only one or at most two per cent in all cities. It is clear that among our successful groups—and their immediate friends—*isolated families are largely a figment of the imagination.*

Table 5

PROPORTIONS OF FAMILIES WITH VARIOUS NUMBERS
OF FRIENDS

City	No friends	One only	Two only	Three only	Four only	Five or more
Boston	1	1	6	7	7	78
New Orleans	1	0*	2	6	5	86
St. Louis	1	2	9	7	9	72
Denver	1	2	8	7	9	74
Omaha	2	2	5	6	9	76
Long Beach	1	3	8	9	9	70

* This figure was two-tenths of a per cent so it was rounded to zero.

THESE FAMILY FRIENDSHIPS ARE LONG-LASTING

It should be emphasized here that these friends are not casual acquaintances. This is evident from Table 6. The students (averaging 18 years of age) had known these family friends within their homes for many years. In the cities of "older settlement" —Boston, New Orleans, and St. Louis—approximately of half the seniors had known these people in their households for 15 years or more.[1] For all cities, from 47 to 73 per cent of the

[1] In this chapter we refer constantly to eastern and older cities, and western and newer cities. We place Boston and New Orleans and St. Louis in the older category and Denver, Omaha and Los Angeles in the newer.

students had known the friend-families more than ten years. Ten years would have been a large share of the knowledgeable lifetime experience of students when, at fifteen or sixteen, they made their educational decision to stay in high school.

Friends known less than ten years followed the familiar pattern of the old city versus the new one. The Boston students had known only 17 per cent of their family friends less than ten years as compared with 53 per cent for Long Beach.

Table 6

LENGTH OF FAMILY FRIENDSHIPS

Percentages of Friendships Lasting

City	0-9 years	10-14 years	15 years or more	More than 10 years
Boston	17	39	44	73
New Orleans	33	13	54	67
St. Louis	36	16	48	64
Denver	42	17	41	58
Omaha	43	15	42	57
Long Beach	53	13	34	47

FAMILY FRIENDS INCLUDE NUMEROUS KINDRED

The length of family friendship does not tell the whole story because, (Table 7), from 29 to 47 per cent of all friends around the homes of these families are "related persons." The relation seemed most often through the marriage of the older children of the family. Thus many kin families are younger than the parental families, with marriages of briefer duration. Conversely, when marriages of brief duration appear, they are likely to be of kin families.

We do this chiefly because the populations residing in them average "older" and "newer" in the time of placement in their present environment. Proof of this is very complicated, but most of it is given definitively in a study entitled "Population Still Moving Westward" in *Metropolitan Statistical Bulletin,* June, 1955.

The shorter experience of the child with such kin-families does not, however, lessen the significance of the friendship relation. Kin are closer, more intimate and better known to the students than non-kin friends. This situation is so important in New Orleans that if the first friend is not related to the family of the student, family behavior tends to reverse itself from the normal, and we have an abnormal family group. This becomes evident when we trace the influence of similarity of friends upon protection of the family against spousal and parent-child estrangement.

KINDRED MOST OFTEN NEAREST FRIENDS

Table 7 shows the proportions of first through fifth friends that were related to the pupil. In every city kindred takes a precedence in nearness of friendship.

Table 7

PROPORTIONS OF KINDRED IN FRIENDSHIP GROUPS

City	First friend	Second friend	Third friend	Fourth friend	Fifth friend	All friends
Boston	44	43	40	33	26	38
New Orleans	54	52	50	41	30	47
St. Louis	49	47	43	36	33	44
Denver	43	42	41	37	31	39
Omaha	43	41	38	36	32	38
Los Angeles	29	34	30	28	26	29

First friends contain more kindred than second friends and so on in order of closeness. Only one irregularity occurs in the whole table, namely that first friends for the Los Angeles families were kindred in only 29 per cent of the cases, as compared with 34 per cent kindred among second friends. Outside of this anomaly, probably due to the newness of the arrival and settlement of the population of Southern California, first friend is kindred more often than second, second more often than third, third more often than fourth, and fourth more often than fifth.

This striking table *should lay at rest the theory that kindred play little or no role in the surroundings of the modern urban family.* As in the previous pages we noted that the isolated family is an anomaly, we now note that kindred play a role in the modern family which exceeds by far any importance paid to it in recent sociological literature.[2]

The legal rights now left to kin are mostly those unbalanced by obligations. Previously the right to control carried with it the obligation to support. But now, if outside kin die intestate—without a will—, the nuclear family has a strong presumption of right to the property left. Then, again, while nuclear family members have no great compulsory duty to support indigent relatives, other than a few poor law administrative practices, the fact of voluntarily supporting these indigent kindred is in many cases recognized as giving the nuclear family right to claim income tax deductions for such acts.

KINDRED RE-EMERGE IN FAMILY "PRIVATE LAW"

The kindred families re-emphasized an old idea—namely that *the family is a legal body of its own.* In the absence of specific legislation of a public nature to the contrary, its will is *law.* Consequently the gathering of kindred about the modern urban family suggests the re-emergence of a private governing body between the state and the family members.[3]

---

[2] A number of important recent studies in England show the high prevalence of kindred in urban family relations there. For London and other English cities see Michael Young and Peter Willmot, *Family and Kinship in East London,* Routledge and Kegan Paul, London, 1957, *passim,* and the recent Unesco 3 volumes, *Studies of the Family,* Ed. Nels Anderson, Gottingen, 1955-57.

[3] Since the beginning of time the role of kin has been fundamental for the protection and psychological conduct of the nuclear family and its members. In most periods of western society, kin had a legal right against, and an obligation to, the nuclear family. In recent times, legal rights have been more or less lost—such as nullification of the right of a mother to enter the home of her daughter or daughter-in-law and to claim support or authority. Another lost right, the ancient unwritten one

The legal principle that the family rules itself is as ancient as western society itself, being stated clearly in the Roman primitive law of the XII Tables (450 B.C.). It was reaffirmed by the great Christian code of family law (*Novellae* of Justinian in 535 A.D.) and gradually worked its way into all of western society through canon law, by which control of the family was placed within the family and which has lasted in one guise or another in most western countries until the past century. The principle has not yet been abrogated; in fact we feel it has recently become largely strengthened. For all socially sanctioned purposes our modern family is becoming again more of a semi-clan and extended family organization.

A second consideration is that the good or successful modern family follows the same principles the older western one did: It uses what kin relations it feels are sympathetic with its purposes and supplements these with non-kin friends. But kin and non-kin alike must be of value to the family or they are rejected. *The "clan," consisting of kindred and clients, still exists and seems restrengthening itself in our cities, but it is now reorganized on a form fitted to modern society.* It is a voluntary and equalitarian social grouping and based upon mutual give and take according to the circumstances. Finally, it is based upon a close coherence of main values, which has the important result of reaffirming the values absorbed by children who see outside life through its eyes.

NON-KIN FRIENDS COME FROM THE NEIGHBORHOOD
OF OTHER FRIENDS

Each pupil told where his parents and their friends had met if the friends were not related to him. Table 8 summarizes the

---

by which a father or father-in-law could claim relationship as an expiation of or excuse for homicide *in flagrante delicto*. While a husband or wife can now generally successfully claim this marital relation as justifying homicide *in flagrante delicto* and thus avoid punishment by a legal fiction, other relatives seldom can. See the development of western law of family rights given in Carle C. Zimmerman *Family and Civilization*, particularly chapters 14-16.

answers under the captions of neighborhood, through other friends, employment, church, social clubs and "other."

Table 8

PLACE OF FIRST MEETING OF SUCCESSFUL FAMILIES AND NON-KINDRED FRIENDS

(Percentages according to situation of meeting)

City	Neighbor-hood	Through other friends	At place of em-ployment	At church	At clubs	In "other" situations
Boston	42	29	9	5	3	12
New Orleans	47	25	11	3	3	12
St. Louis	38	25	12	10	5	10
Denver	38	22	17	10	4	9
Omaha	40	21	15	9	5	10
Los Angeles	39	19	15	9	4	14

In every case in every city, "neighborhood" played the dominant role in the meeting of non-kin friends. This is followed by the influence of the introduction by mutual friends. Work, church, clubs and other forms of making friendship were relatively unimportant, considered as places of meeting.

However, we must not let Table 8 give a biased view of the situation because even though few persons made their friends through the place of employment and the church, nevertheless they picked friends closely like them in economic status and in religious faith. These relationships will be enlarged upon in later chapters on the selection of friends according to likenesses, and the decisive significance of this principle for family protection.

From this law, the tables have begun to show a close-knit group of relationships. In Boston 38 per cent of all families about the home were kindred, of the others 71 per cent were from the neighborhood or through introductions by mutual friends. This means that 82 per cent of all friends in Boston were very close to the parental families. In New Orleans kindred, neighbors and other friends accounted for 85 per cent of the family friends; in

St. Louis, 79 per cent; in Denver, 76 per cent; in Omaha, 76 per cent; and even in the newest organized city, the Long Beach section of Los Angeles, 70 per cent.

Again we emphasize what is becoming more and more apparent in this study, namely that these family friendships are made very carefully to form circles of trust and intimacy. The first order is predominantly kindred either by blood or inter-marriage. The second is the neighborhood and the third comes through introduction by other friends. Since, as reported in Table 6, most of the acquaintanceships had already lasted more than ten years, and two-fifths of them more than fifteen years, we must

Table 9

LENGTH OF MARRIAGES OF PARENTAL AND FRIEND-FAMILIES

Percentages by Groups

City and Families	Up to 9 years	10-14 years	15 or more years
Boston			
Students	3	3	94
Friends	19	18	63
New Orleans			
Students	3	2	95
Friends	19	18	63
St. Louis			
Students	7	4	89
Friends	22	18	60
Denver			
Students	7	5	88
Friends	22	21	57
Omaha			
Students	7	4	89
Friends	24	18	58
Los Angeles			
Students	13	7	80
Friends	26	19	55

Table 10

NUMBER OF CHILDREN IN THE FAMILIES AND THEIR FRIENDS

Percentage Distribution

City	None	One	Two	Three or more
Boston				
Students	—	10	22	68
Friends	11	15	26	48
New Orleans				
Students	—	14	28	58
Friends	13	19	28	40
St. Louis				
Students	—	13	26	61
Friends	15	18	26	41
Denver				
Students	—	12	30	58
Friends	14	18	29	39
Omaha				
Students	—	12	25	63
Friends	12	16	28	44
Los Angeles				
Students	—	21	36	43
Friends	15	23	32	30

consider them a tremendous part of the psychological walls about the child, beginning early in his life and lasting through his teen-age problem years.

FAMILY FRIENDS REPRESENT A PANORAMA OF SUCCESS

In Tables 9 and 10 we give a resume of the years of marriage of the parental and friend-families and number of children in each. The purpose of these two tables are several. First, we wish to describe the friend-families in terms of the variant ages of persons seen in the homes of the teen-ager. The child's own family is a mature one. Nearly all its children have been born (most of the parents had been married twenty years or more), and the parents are forty years of age or better. The friend-families are younger, and in them the student sees a variant section of the life cycle.

The friend-families give the student a panorama of what he has not yet lived himself but which he will soon approach. That is, he sees younger married couples, ten to fifteen per cent of whom are yet childless, and in the first stage of the life cycle of the family. He has a preview of what he would soon be going through if he found a job, or completed his higher education, and then formed a family by his own marriage.

He also sees from fifteen to twenty-three per cent of his parental friends in the business of rearing a first child, and twenty-six to thirty-two per cent who have their second child and are that much farther advanced toward "a completed family." The remainder, thirty to forty-eight per cent, have three or more children and, in essence, are essentially full formed or mature families.

This panorama of life, from the family point of view, which the child sees within his own home, is a sort of "family training school." One of the complaints about "family sociology" is that it teaches the young about getting married but says little about the ensuing problems for the next forty years.

Wholly different is the voluntaristic and "natural-life" training for families which occurs within the good families and their intimate friends. Within the circle of this small intimate group the child gets a first-hand introduction to family life from cradle to the grave, from diaper to the shroud.

THE "GOOD" FAMILY REPRODUCES ITSELF

A second aspect is the coinciding of the cultural and the physical aspects of the family. These family groups present two pictures of life to the child. We have spoken in an earlier work of the dual field aspect of family life, its cultural and its biological significance.[4] Not only are these families showing their ability to

---

[4] See Zimmerman and Cervantes, *Marriage and the Family,* Chapter III.

produce children who complete their high school educations—
successful or "civilization-adequate" as we call them here—but
also most of them are, or are becoming, adequate biologically in
that they are reproducers.

In a civilization with high tensions such as ours, not all persons can become parents and not all can reach the reproducing
rate of three or more children. But these we are studying either
have done so or are embarked upon a course leading to it.

Becoming a parent is more than a biological act. It involves
the will-power and determination to overcome modern vicissitudes,
and to undertake and carry out a long-time obligation to rear a
child or children properly through our now doubled and expensive nonage period. Nowadays a parent enters upon a long and
expensive undertaking that includes not only rearing the child
physically but seeing him through an enlarged educational career.
Families that do this are different from those that do not, at
least in respect to greater determination. They seem to have
greater optimism about the future, better fortune and more
psycho-biological capacity.

IT PRESENTS ITS CHILDREN AN OPTIMISTIC VIEW OF LIFE

In a large degree, the panorama of life, given as training experience to the child in such a good family system as this, is a
selective one. The student is very much secluded from first-hand
experience with all the failures of family life, those springing from
lack of determination, defeatism and poor fortune. A panoramic
experience with failure, if he were not shielded from it, would
tend to weaken the attitudes of the child towards the family system, and he would be pushed more toward the existentialist
attitude of a non-moral evaluation of different ways of life.

FAMILY FRIENDS MAKE A "CLOSED" SOCIAL SYSTEM

Thus the good family system is selective. It shows only "good"
to its children insofar as it can control the intimate surroundings
of the home.

This selected panorama of life-training makes the good family and its friends a sort of "civilization-adequate closed social system" about the lives of the children. It includes positive elements and excludes negative; these young students are unconsciously moulded. As shown later, the same methods are extended to the full family environment. All elements of life contrary to "good family" processes are excluded, and children are kept away from a first-hand knowledge of failures in life.

Here we note again that the older cities do this more adequately than the most recently settled cities of the West. While the statistics are somewhat irregular, there is, in general, a constant tendency for the American urban social systems in all regions to "settle down" on a permanent-civilization basis. Probably the older cities have done this more than the newer, but the same processes are evident in both.

BROKEN FAMILIES MORE FREQUENT IN THE NEWER CITIES

Table 11 gives the details about first and subsequent marriages of the students' parents and their friend-families. It does not, as does a later table, distinguish between remarriages following the death of one of the spouses, and those following divorce. Since the American divorce rate is higher in the West than the East, and in the newer cities as compared with the old, the rates for "first marriage only" decrease as we move from East to West and from the older to the newer cities.[5]

Students' parents were married only once in 91.4 per cent of the cases in Boston. This figure decreases steadily as we move through our list of cities to 74.5 per cent in Los Angeles. The

---

[5] We constantly use the idea that the rates for marital dissolutions by divorce or annulment (which is now largely divorce by legal fiction) grow progressively as one moves from the older and eastern cities toward the newer and western ones. Divorce and annulment statistics in the United States are so numerous and so detailed that they only confuse anyone who attempts to cite or to study them but the points discussed above are made clear by Paul H. Jacobson in his article "Marriage Dissolutions in New York State in Relation to Their Trend in the United States," *Millbank Memorial Fund Quarterly*, January, 1950.

Table 11

REMARRIAGES OF FAMILIES AND FRIENDS

| City | Percentages | | | Percentages of subsequent marriage for: | |
	First marriage	Subsequent marriage	Both	Mother only	Father only
Boston:					
Students	91.4	8.7	2.3	2.2	3.7
Friends	87.7	12.3	3.9	5.1	3.3
New Orleans:					
Students	89.7	10.3	3.6	3.1	3.6
Friends	87.6	12.6	4.0	4.1	4.5
St. Louis:					
Students	85.2	14.8	5.9	4.1	4.8
Friends	82.4	17.6	7.2	5.1	5.3
Denver:					
Students	83.4	16.6	6.2	4.8	5.6
Friends	81.0	19.0	8.2	5.5	5.3
Omaha:					
Students	82.1	16.9	7.7	4.9	4.3
Friends	84.5	15.5	7.4	4.3	2.8
Los Angeles:					
Students	74.5	25.5	10.6	10.0	5.0
Friends	77.3	22.7	8.9	8.2	5.6

same decrease is noted among the friend-families. Thus the rate moves from 87.7 per cent first marriages for friend-families in Boston to 77.3 per cent among friend-families in the Long Beach section of Los Angeles.

INCREASED BROKEN FAMILIES MEANS HIGHER "AVOIDANCE" TENDENCIES

A fact of importance is the decrease of remarried friends around the families in Los Angeles and in Omaha. Generally in the cities with a low divorce rate (the older ones), the parental families associated with remarried families more freely than in the newer cities with higher divorce rates. That is, in the East more friends were remarried than parents; in Omaha and Los Angeles, fewer friends were remarried than parents.

In Boston the parents were remarried in 8.7 per cent of the cases, but their friends in 12.3 per cent of the cases. In Los Angeles, parents were remarried in 25.5 per cent of the cases, but the friends in only 22.7. In the West and the newer cities, *where broken families are more frequent, the students' families avoided them more rigidly* than in the East and in the older cities.

We do not know for sure why this is. We think *families in the high divorce cities tried to avoid having remarried friends.* As this is a consistent factor, it seems worth comment. It may have something to do with a theory of "limits." That is, where remarriages are fewer and more commonly on account of the death of a spouse, people accept the remarried friends and kindred more willingly. But when remarriages are more numerous and because of divorce, there seems a tendency toward rejection.

A remarriage is not as much a bar to social acceptance in "good families" in Boston, New Orleans, St. Louis and strange to say, Denver, as in Omaha and Los Angeles. These last two are cities of more troubled families and desertion among students' families and juvenile arrest records.

What we are really measuring, in all probability, is the greater pains taken by student families to keep their homes free from "broken home" associations in cities where there are very large numbers of broken homes. This is a natural reaction. When burglaries break out in a heretofore peaceful community, all at once people begin to pay more attention to locks and bolts.

CONCEALMENT OF REMARRIAGES DECREASES "AVOIDANCE"

This greater avoidance idea is borne out by a careful consideration of remarriages among friends when the remarriage concerned "both parents," the "mothers only" or "fathers only."

In Boston, the percentages for the three categories are small, and do not greatly differ. The same is true for New Orleans, St. Louis and Denver, cities with a generally slightly higher broken-family rate than Boston, but still not extreme. But in Omaha and Los Angeles, the situation is sharply different, with the percentages higher for "both parents" and "mothers only" than for "fathers only." If both parents in a family are remarried, or the mother only, the signs of a former broken family are hard to conceal. Consequently avoidance of them is greater in the newer cities than of families where the father is in a second marriage and the break is not so obvious. The mother who remarries brings with her the children of a previous marriage. The father if he remarries generally has in his household only the children of his second or later marriage.

It must be made clear, however, that broken spousal relations as discussed here are not solely in the divorce or desertion categories. No one can be blamed if a spouse is dead; and in the great majority of cases, mothers left with dependent children by divorced fathers have made the best choice they thought possible in remarrying and trying to bring up their children in a completed home. Since these divorced mothers are the very ones who know most about the possibilities of a father's example being passed onto a child, then these might be the very persons who, in the high-divorce-rate cities, take precautions to avoid association with friends who have had similar breakage of earlier homes. As our analysis proceeds we will recur to this theme of reversal in the newer cities.

We should also caution here again that our analysis is not of "all families" but only of good families. This should be remembered throughout this study. To rephrase what has been said earlier, we do not know what all families, or poor families, do, except by inference, and this type of sociological analysis of the "good" or civilization-adequate people, doesn't deal with the others.

DIVORCE, DESERTION AND JUVENILE ARREST INCREASE IN WESTERN AND NEWER CITIES

Now we turn to the proportions of families with records of a divorce or desertion. These are data on both estrangement between the parents and also between parents and children due to police arrests. (The latter means that at least once the police had had to discipline a child by making an arrest.) Here we present the facts by city, leaving the analysis until later.

Table 12

FAMILIES WITH A RECORD OF DIVORCE OR DESERTION

Per cents with Divorced or Deserted Histories

City	Student families	Friend-families
Boston	6.0	6.2
New Orleans	6.3	5.5
St. Louis	10.2	8.0
Denver	9.3	8.0
Omaha	10.6	7.5
Los Angeles	15.8	11.3

The newer cities have higher rates for divorce and desertion as well as juvenile arrest among both families and their friends than had the older ones.[6] The increase is not regular and has some variations, but it exists.

FEWER FRIEND THAN STUDENT FAMILIES WERE BROKEN

Student families, with only one exception, had higher rates for divorce and desertion and for juvenile arrests than did the friend-families. The exception is Boston, where divorce or desertion occurred in 6 per cent of student families and 6.2 of friend families. This takes us back to the argument in the previous section where we noted a tendency to avoid family breakage more rigidly in the cities where it was high. However, whether that is

---

[6] The correlation between husband-wife estrangements rates and parent-child difficulties (interference by police between parent and child) has been studied intensively here at Harvard and the reference to Zimmerman-Cervantes, *op. cit.*, gives the outstanding results.

true or not true, it is really true that families, broken or un
broken, try to have family friends where possible, of the unbroke
variety.

We shall come back to this theme in later chapters.

SUMMARY OF FRIENDSHIP GROUPINGS

This chapter summarizes some basic facts about the familie
of the high school seniors and their friends. Only a few—one pe
cent in most cities—reported no friends at all, while *from 70 t*
86 per cent claimed and reported about five or more intima
family-group friends. Most of the friends had been coming int
the houses of the students for more than ten years. Apparentl
among successful families, the isolated individual family is th
extreme exception—not the rule.

Kindred constituted from three-tenths to almost a half, of th
friend families, depending upon the city. Kindred were the close
friends in every rank of friendship up to five, which is as far a
our study went. The idea that people in the modern America
cities no longer know and associate with their kindred is seem
ingly put to rest. Non-kindred friends, in most cases, were met i
the immediate neighborhood or through other friends. From 7
to 82 per cent of all family friends in all cities were either kindre
neighbors or close friends of friends.

The friends who visited in the homes of the students *were*
different stages of the family life cycle. Some friends of the paren
were yet childless, some had only one child and some only tw
The students' parents were older and generally had reached th
maturity of their family life cycles. In nearly every case all
their expected children had been born. This diversity of frien
families meant that *the student saw a panorama of the tradition*
good family life cycle in his home. He formed a close acquai
tanceship with "good" family life and its problems from th
cradle to the grave. Since the friends are also good or civilizatio
adequate from the standpoint of reproduction, the closed soci
system of the student's family and their friends gave the stude

an extremely long training in family activity and behavior. The type of family social system in which the pupil was raised seemed to be a controlling influence upon his major attitudes towards life.

AVERSION TO BROKEN HOMES IS GENERAL

From nine to twenty-five per cent of the students were living in families in which the father or mother or both had made a subsequent marriage. Some were due to the deaths of spouses, others to divorce. Death seemed a more important factor in remarriages of families of this good type in the older cities and in the East. *In the newer cities and in the West divorce as a cause of remarriage of parents in student homes was more dominant.* This is in accord with the much higher divorce rates in many of the newer cities and the Western states.

In the East and in the older cities student families associated with friends which had slightly higher rates for subsequent marriage than in the students' families themselves. This may have been because remarriage of widows and widowers is not viewed in quite the same light as remarriage arising from divorce. However, as we show later, aversion to divorce is not as important as a general avoidance of broken homes as such.

In the West and in the newer cities where divorce is more frequent, families seemed to fear direct intimate association within their homes with remarried persons more so than in the East and older cities. Thus apparently when conditions become difficult from this point of view good families *try* to isolate themselves more from the other type. In other words, "polarization" between family types increases. Avoidance of intimate association with remarried families becomes very marked in cities where the divorce rate is extremely high.

The analysis of this practice is introduced here to point out, and to lead up to eventually testing the hypothesis that the family-friend groups are connected very closely with attempts by parents to control the child's environment. The groups are felt by the parents to be highly significant for the child's character control.

THE PROBLEM OF REMARRIAGE

The fact of social avoidance of remarried families in citi
where remarriage is frequent is true for "subsequent marriages
in which "both parents" have remarried, and those in which th
"woman only" is remarried. When "fathers only" are remarrie
avoidance is less marked. As was suggested earlier, this reflect
we think, the general procedure in child custody. In ninety po
cent of divorces in America the custody of the children remair
with the mother, which means that when mothers remarry the
bring with them the children by the first husband.

Thus the family where the mother is remarried consists o
husband, wife, mother and her children. It is not the standar
husband-wife, parents-children type. Other children may b
added but the relation between father and the first husband'
children is an artificial one. In a later chapter we will deal wit
the difficulties of being a step-father as reflected in juvenile arre
rates. When a father remarries a hitherto unmarried woman, th
children are his and hers and this is apparently not looked upc
with as much general suspicion. This father-remarried family cor
sists generally of only husband and wife, parents and the
children.

Whereas some of the families studied were troubled by divorc
and juvenile arrest in every city, the rates generally were sign
ficantly lower than those of the general populations of thes
cities.[7] This introduces an idea already suggested several times i

---

[7] We do not prove this here but it is obvious. Divorce statistics a
very unreliable by districts because of the migratory divorce situation,
which divorces are secured in "foreign" jurisdictions. California reports
1951 one divorce for every two marriages, but in Los Angeles the ci
papers record daily a list of divorces generally nearly equalling in numb
marriage licenses. Juvenile delinquency statistics are also treacherous eve
by districts or the country as a whole, because arrest rates are not report
when intercession by parents or friends keep the cases from court actio
Even the Senate Committee on Juvenile Delinquency merely estimates th
arrest rate as a multiple factor of reported court trials of juveniles. C
some of these statistical details, plus proof that parent-child difficulti
parallel those of husband and wife, see Zimmerman and Cervantes, Ma
riage and The Family, already cited.

s work, and one which will be developed further as we pro-
d: that good families are adequate from both the cultural and
logical points of view. Thus we reaffirm what is called the
ıal field" nature of the family. It is both an individual and
tural institution.

FAMILY FRIENDSHIP GROUPS:
KEEP STRANGERS OUT

chapter IV MANY TYPES OF SOCIAL GROUPINGS ARE TO BE FOUN
Some are formal; others informal. Some are lar
others small. Some confer status, such as the family; the a
others have is legal perpetuity, such as the corporation. In som
the members must come face to face; in others, not. Some are r
lated to characteristics of all human beings, and some have speci
ends. Our study deals with only two group problems—the i
formal groups of intimate friends about the family and the rel
tion of these to the family.

In the present chapter, we meant to inspect the cumulati
nature of these friendship groupings, which tends to make the
into what we call "a closed social system." By "cumulative n
ture" we mean that each of the friends tends to have a *conside*
able number of things in common with the others in his grou
Each different group follows this same principle: Strangers a
Strangeness Keep Out.

A "simple group" is one in which the members have only o
or a few things in common, such as a collective interest
fishing, in baseball or in having a street repaired. In such a grou
the individual and collective mentalities of the members a
closely alike, with many common interests.

We have already shown that family friends were often kindr
by blood or marriage, that they often came from the same regio
of origin and that they were generally in the same income grou
ings. We have also shown there is a tendency among fami
friendship groups to share a similar religious faith or confessi
as a fundamental common interest. One reason for this is becau
religious faiths generally have unique familistic doctrines
practices. Similar professions of faith mean, in most cases, n
only common theological and social commitments but likewi
similar basic attitudes in regard to family practices.

Before we begin to study the influence of friendship groups)on the family—upon its husband-wife relationship, upon its *rent-child solidarity and upon its "walls" of common values *out the teen-agers—we want to describe and to show the *mulative nature of these family-friendship groups. Our aim in *is chapter is to show how the friend group opens itself and *troduces the family members to the outside world, only when *cessary, and then closes these doors against strangeness.

*MULATIVE NATURE OF FAMILY FRIENDSHIPS

Table 13

ST. LOUIS: CUMULATIVE NATURE OF FRIENDSHIP GROUPS*
(Number of Traits in Common Between Parental and Friend-Families)

Percentages with common traits by rank of friends

*mber of *its	First friend	Second friend	Third friend	Fourth friend	Fifth friend	All friends
)ne	4.5	5.5	7.6	8.9	9.0	6.9
ne only	16.4	17.8	18.5	20.4	22.2	18.7
vo only	29.8	30.5	32.4	35.9	33.2	31.7
*ree only	34.6	32.4	29.1	27.2	27.0	30.2
*l four	15.7	13.8	12.4	10.6	8.6	12.5
)tal	100.0	100.0	100.0	100.0	100.0	100.0

Common traits are income, religion, region of origin and kin.

Table 13 shows the percentages of the families of the high *hool seniors which have none, one, two, three or all four of the dices of similarity in common with their friends. The friends are ranged by nearness to the family from 1-5. The four indices of nilarity used are income, religious faith, region of origin of *sbands and kinship. The friends may have many other things common but we use only these gross indices of similarity be- *een them. The data from St. Louis (Table 13) are generally pical of the pattern found in each of the cities studied.

Our presupposition is that even persons with none of these

things in common have many interests with their friends—otherwise they would not be friends. But if one or more of these above four traits is shared with their friends, we may presume that much more is held in common than when none is shared.

To repeat, if friends are from the same region, their wives have the same religious faith, if they are at about the same income level, and if they are kindred, we believe that they have *very* many ties in common. Where friends have four similarities we believe their ties are closer than in the case where a lesser number of these indices of similarity are present.

The friends are arranged in rank of nearness to the student families, so we can study close friends in relation to far-away friends or friend one with two, two with three and so on. Near friends are most often around the houses. If they are more like the families than far friends then the cumulativity of similar value is greater.

One of the first conclusions we reach is that friendship as measured by these four social traits, economics, faith, origin and kin is *cumulative*. In the whole study of more than a quarter million persons less than one friend in ten had nothing in common with the parents of the seniors as measured by these indices.

Table 14

BOSTON: CUMULATIVE NATURE OF FRIENDSHIP GROUPS*
(Number of Traits in Common Between Parental and Friend-Families)

Percentages with common traits by rank of friends

Number of traits	First friend	Second friend	Third friend	Fourth friend	Fifth friend	All friends
None	3.1	4.7	5.3	7.1	7.3	5.4
One only	16.8	17.2	18.8	20.0	20.6	18.6
Two only	31.8	31.3	34.1	33.6	38.2	33.6
Three only	36.1	34.0	31.5	31.1	26.8	32.1
All four	12.2	12.8	10.3	8.2	7.1	10.3
Total	100.0	100.0	100.0	100.0	100.0	100.0

* Common traits are income, religion, region of origin and kin.

In the older cities of Boston (Table 14), New Orleans (Table 15), and St. Louis (Table 13), only about one friend in twenty had none of the four traits in common with the parents. In the newer cities of Denver (Table 16), Omaha (Table 17) and Los Angeles (Table 18), the friends with no index in common with the parents of students scarcely amounted to one in ten. Thus the good family is generally surrounded with "closely like" friends.

Table 15

NEW ORLEANS: CUMULATIVE NATURE OF FRIENDSHIP GROUPS*
(Number of Traits in Common Between Parental and Friend-Families)

Percentages with common traits by rank of friends

Number of traits	First friend	Second friend	Third friend	Fourth friend	Fifth friend	All friends
None	2.2	3.6	3.3	3.9	5.0	3.6
One only	9.5	9.4	11.6	13.1	13.4	11.3
Two only	27.9	30.6	31.9	32.9	32.2	31.0
Three only	41.5	40.8	36.8	37.2	37.0	38.7
All four	18.9	15.6	16.4	12.9	12.4	15.4
Total	100.0	100.0	100.0	100.0	100.0	100.0

* Common traits are income, religion, region of origin and kin.

Table 16

DENVER: CUMULATIVE NATURE OF FRIENDSHIP GROUPS*
(Number of Traits in Common Between Parental and Friend-Families)

Percentages with common traits by rank of friends

Number of traits	First friend	Second friend	Third friend	Fourth friend	Fifth friend	All friends
None	7.1	9.4	11.7	11.1	15.4	10.7
One only	24.7	24.8	23.8	28.0	27.7	25.6
Two only	32.8	32.0	31.7	32.3	28.7	31.6
Three only	25.2	23.0	24.1	21.0	20.8	23.0
All four	10.2	10.8	8.7	7.6	7.4	9.1
Total	100.0	100.0	100.0	100.0	100.0	100.0

* Common traits are income, religion, region of origin and kin.

Table 17

OMAHA: CUMULATIVE NATURE OF FRIENDSHIP GROUPS*
(Number of Traits in Common Between Parental and Friend-Families)

Percentages with common traits by rank of friends

Number of traits	First friend	Second friend	Third friend	Fourth friend	Fifth friend	All friends
None	6.9	9.3	8.2	10.0	11.2	8.9
One only	16.1	19.4	21.0	21.7	23.8	19.9
Two only	32.6	31.5	34.4	32.3	34.6	32.9
Three only	32.3	28.9	27.2	27.7	22.8	28.3
All four	12.1	10.9	9.2	8.3	7.6	10.0
Total	100.0	100.0	100.0	100.0	100.0	100.0

* Common traits are income, religion, region of origin and kin.

Table 18

LONG BEACH: CUMULATIVE NATURE OF FRIENDSHIP GROUPS*
(Number of Traits in Common Between Parental and Friend-Families)

Percentages with common traits by rank of friends

Number of traits	First friend	Second friend	Third friend	Fourth friend	Fifth friend	All friends
None	12.8	16.4	15.2	15.9	19.4	15.7
One only	32.7	29.2	32.2	33.1	30.1	31.4
Two only	30.2	30.8	31.3	31.2	31.7	30.9
Three only	18.5	18.2	16.2	15.7	15.1	16.9
All four	5.9	5.5	5.2	4.2	3.8	5.0
Total	100.0	100.0	100.0	100.0	100.0	100.0

* Common traits are income, religion, region of origin and kin.

FRIENDS IN OLDER CITIES HAVE MOST IN COMMON

The second conclusion concerns the proportions of families with all four measured traits in common with their friends. The general tendency in the older cities was for the proportions of families with all four traits in common with their friends to be

wice as high as those with no measured trait in common. In
Boston (Table 14) 5.4 per cent of all friends had no trait in
ommon with the student parents but 10.3 per cent had all four
ogether.

St. Louis friends had no trait in common with parents of
tudents in only 6.9 per cent of the cases, but all four in 12.5
per cent. Thus the families with the maximum measured traits in
ommon nearly always were twice as frequent as minimum cases
n the older cities. So we may now say that the trend in the older
ities is for families of the good type to increase the proportions
f good families about them.

In the newer cities the analysis shows that maximum per-
entages (four traits in common) nearly always about equals the
minimum figures. For instance in Denver (Table 16), 10.7 per
ent of the friend-families were those with no measured trait in
ommon whereas in that same city 9.1 per cent had all four in
ommon. In Omaha (Table 17), 8.9 per cent had none whereas
0.0 held all four traits mutually.

Thirdly, we point out and *emphasize the extreme selectivity
of friendship choice in terms of common interests.* In St. Louis,
12.5 per cent of all friends had the four traits in common with
he student families. This means that of friends, one out of eight
vas not only in the same economic class but had the same re-
igious confession, the same basic region of origin and were
kindred by blood or marriage. This cumulative fact concerns the
relations among more than fifteen thousand families in and
around the high schools of a large city which has nearly a million
persons in its central zone. The people in St. Louis are both
vhite and colored and from all regions of the United States. Also
he city includes large proportions of older and newer arrivals
rom all the European countries

Similarity in economic groups in itself is a high selective
achievement since there are diverse age and life cycle positions
for the friend-families as contrasted with the student families. But
added to that we have the similarity of religious faith, regions of
origin and of kindred or intermarriage.

The significance of cumulativity of likeness among frienc families is shown most strikingly in Table 19 by the proportion of all friends by city with two or more of the measured traits i common.

Table 19

FRIEND-FAMILIES WITH TWO OR MORE TRAITS IN COMMON*

City	Percentage of friend families with two or more traits in common
Boston	76
New Orleans	85
St. Louis	74
Denver	64
Omaha	71
Los Angeles	53

* Common traits are income, religion, region of origin and kinship.

Thus a family and its friends makes a small closed socia system because of all the people physically available to its doors only a few, those remarkably like the family itself, are admitte to the system. Others are excluded from such intimacy.

THE CLOSEST FRIENDS ARE MOST ALIKE

This cumulativity of friendship or its closed nature, with it capacity to impress a system of similar values upon the children is further emphasized by the greater likeness between their par ents and the first and most intimate friends, as opposed to lesse likenesses between the parents and the subsequent friends. With out exception the comparisons show the *parents have more in common with first friends* than second, second than third, third than fourth and fourth than fifth. The child or children see the first friend more often and over a longer period of years than the second or lesser intimate friends.

This may be demonstrated by comparing the first and fifth friends for each city according to the proportions of these with

ll measured indices in common with the parents, and the proportions with two or more indices in common (Table 20). St.

Table 20

CLOSENESS OF FRIENDSHIP
AND NUMBER OF COMMON INTERESTS*

Percentages of

City	First friends with all four traits in common	Fifth friends with all four traits in common	First friends with two or more traits in common	Fifth friends with two or more traits in common
Boston	12.2	7.1	80	72
New Orleans	18.9	12.4	88	82
St. Louis	15.7	8.6	79	69
Denver	10.2	7.4	68	57
Omaha	12.1	7.6	77	65
Los Angeles	5.9	2.8	55	51

* As measured by economic class, region of origin of fathers, religion of mothers and kindred by blood or marriage.

Louis, for instance, shows 15.7 per cent of the first friends with all indices in common with the students' parents. Only 8.6 per cent of the fifth rank of friend families had all things in common with their parents. In St. Louis also, 79 per cent of all friends of the first order had at least two indices in common with the parents as contrasted with only 69 per cent of the fifth order with two indices in common with the students' parents.

We have shown that divorce, desertion and juvenile arrest histories were more prevalent among student families of Omaha and the Long Beach Section of Los Angeles than among those of the other cities. It was also shown for these cities that they reversed some of the trends for the newer cities as against the older. Successful families in Omaha and Los Angeles appear *more* exclusive (and closed) than in the older cities and in the East. *"Society" is more open in the West than in the East but family groups try to be more "closed" in the West than in the East.*

The older cities, with lower divorce, desertion and juvenil arrest records among the high school populations, had about th same or only a slightly lower proportion of troubled familie among their friends than in the students' families. On the othe hand, in Omaha and Los Angeles where divorce, desertion an arrest histories were much higher in the student population fami lies, the tendency seemed to be for the good families to close i very severely and to try to avoid contact with the troubled one:

It is possible that the higher rates for likeness in Omaha tha in Denver, as measured in Table 20, is a reflection of a tren toward a greater polarization of families in the West and newe cities where the stresses are greater. However, this reversal in th selection of friends in the West by this particular index of likenes is not carried out in Los Angeles. If such a tendency is unde way there, it was not evident at the time of the study due perhap to the newness and mobility of the population in Souther California.

THE FRIEND-FAMILIES DO NOT OVERLAP

Two other processes are important in an understanding of th significance of cumulative likenesses among families and thei friends and the wall of psychological protection thrown about th child and his home by this system of organization. One is that th *"other friends" of friends of a family are generally not the sam as the "other friends" of a student family.*

This may be explained as follows. Friend *one* of a studen family has generally five or six close friends of its own. Bu generally these *do not include* friends two, three, four and fiv of the student family. Some overlapping exists but not much.

Friends two, three, four and five of the student family *may b* included as intimates of friend one, or one or more of them ma be, but as a general rule a student family, with its five friends, i not an exclusive, self-contained, autonomous group. This is be cause the five friends each have five or more friends, and th overlapping is only about one friend or less. Six families wit completely exclusive friends, except one, would make a ring o interlocking social relationships embracing thirty-one families. Six families with non-exclusive friends (who were all friends of only each other) would make a highly ingrown autonomous group of only six friends).

The differences between the six and the thirty-one families is very important. If only six friends had all friendships and relations with each other, the families of each would have few roots in the world and the avenues of intimate knowledge of the individual family with the outside world of strangers would be very limited and not broad and extensive.

It would be almost impossible for the modern family to meet the world successfully if it were circumscribed into an isolated-overlapping-small community of five or six friends. The families we have studied have been successful above the average in meeting the world on a civilization-adequate level of behavior and under extremely difficult circumstances. This is evident throughout this work. One of the means has been by embedding themselves in an extensive, as well as an intensive, system of communication with, understanding of, and ways of grappling with, a large and varied universe. The intensive part is the five family friends; the extensive part is the twenty-five "other" friends—friends of family friends.

FRIEND-FAMILIES MAKE AN EXTENSIVE AS WELL AS AN INTENSIVE SOCIAL SYSTEM

We do not mean to say here that a family does not know the intimate friends of its friends. It does know them (as far-away friends) (farther than the sixth) and as "acquaintances." It hears a good deal about them in intimate gossip, but, except at infrequent and large gatherings, does not ordinarily meet commonly and intimately with them.

However, there is some tendency towards overlapping of friendship groups. We have already noted that the introduction of friends by other friends was an important factor in forming intimate acquaintanceships. However, of the important factors leading to discovering friendship families which we listed, kinship, community or neighborhood residence, and other meeting conditions, "friends introducing friends" came toward the last. This means a limited overlapping of friend groups, but only a limited one.

Our estimates, therefore, as to the skein of relationships around a family, is neither five friends only, nor thirty, but rather twenty-five. By this we mean that in the system of student family A and its five closest friends, and the five closest friends of the friends of family A, there are about twenty-five separate families involved. In case of an emergency in family A, it has the chance to counsel not only with its five friends, B, C, D, E, and F but also, through them, with their friends.

On the average, as we have suggested, the group is about twenty-five. However, we find that family A seldom approaches directly a friend of B, C, D, E, and F but goes to his B, C, D, E, or F friends, and the latter intercede with *their* friends for the benefit of family A.

Here is how the typical situation seems to work. Family A goes to Family B for help. A and B families are first-rank friends. It makes no difference what the quest is about, a position for a child, a summer job, some difficulty in school, college entrance examinations, income tax advice or what not. Family B oftentimes finds that it has not the information, the connections or the where-with-all to meet family A's need. However, B has a friend whom we will designate as H who is known to A, but not intimately, but is very close to B. B goes to H and gets the information, advice, or help which A requires. This situation or others like it is repeated over and over again. Thereby family A by being close to B and to C, D, E and F, has available to him from time to time about twenty-five other families for occasional help.

FRIENDS-FRIENDS HAVE THE SAME VALUES AS DO THE PARENTS

Now this is beginning to become involved. However, all we are saying is that the values of the A group of friends are closely similar to those of the largely separate B, C, D, E and F oriented groups of friends. We shall present the proofs of this in detail in later chapters, but it needs to be stated summarily now.

The proof is that when a given group of A's associate with B's, C's, D's, E's and F's who are like them, the A's gain in protection from the association. This is measured by reduced divorce, desertion and juvenile-arrest history rates in the A families. As we shall show later for every city, families with friends like them have lower rates for desertion, divorce, and juvenile-arrest histories than families which associate with friends unlike them.

But that is only one side of the case. The B's, C's, D's, E's and F's gain also from this association with A, in lower rates for juvenile arrest and divorces and desertions. This is because they not only associate with the A family but with other families, in addition B's, C's, D's, E's and F's themselves, who resemble them in major familial values. Friendships are influenced not only by major values but by *tastes*. For example, the friend of B, who is not A, C, D, E or F, tends to have major values and tastes like those of A. Here common values and tastes influence the intimacy.

In other words, the social systems of family friendships made by families B, C, D, E and F, is similar to that of A. That is, the close friends of B may be denoted in this manner: B has G for its first friend. Its second friend is A (from the first family group). Then it has friends H, I, and either J, a new family, or one of the original C, D, E and F, if there is any overlapping. *Thus there is an astonishing similarity of basic values in the friend groups and the friends-friend groups.* This makes for an extensive social system of about twenty-five families which bulwarks and stands by the intensive family system of five or six families.

ILLUSTRATION OF SIMILAR VALUES IN THE EXTENSIVE AND INTENSIVE FAMILY SYSTEMS

To make this clearer we will illustrate it by some figures from St. Louis, Mo. There we studied 2,526 student families which are our A's. They had 2,511 first friends (B's), 2,449 second friends (C's), 2,182 third friends (D's), 1,993 fourth friends (E's), and 1,835 fifth friends (F's).

When some of the A's associate with some of the B's with whom they have none of our four traits in common (economics, faith, origin and kin), these A's have juvenile-arrest rates of 12.4 per cent, and divorce and desertion rates of 19.5 per cent.

However, when others of the A's associate with others of the B's with whom they have all four traits in common, the juvenile-arrest rate of the A families drops to 7.8 per cent and the divorce and desertion rate to 6.3 per cent.

The same is true of B families. Those B families which associate with A families with whom they have none of the four traits in common, have juvenile-arrest rates of 15 per cent and divorce or desertion rates of 20.4 per cent. But B families that associate with the A's who have all four traits in common have juvenile-arrest rates of only 2.8 per cent and divorce or desertion rates of 3.3 per cent. Putting this in a semi-tabular form makes it look as follows.

Of 2,526 student families (A's) in St. Louis, 113 associated with 113 B families (first friends) with whom they had no common grounds as measured by economic status, religion, origin or kinship. These 113 families of students had 14 divorce or desertion histories and 22 arrest histories or 12.4 and 19.5 on a percentage basis.

The same 113 B families (or first friend-families) had 23 divorces or desertions and 17 arrests, or percentages of 20.4 and 15.0.

Three hundred and ninety-five student families (A's) in St. Louis associated with 395 B families with whom they had four common grounds. The 395 A families had had 25 divorces or desertions and 31 arrest histories or percentages of 6.3 and 7.8.

The 395 B families with four traits in common had had 13 divorces or desertions and 11 arrest histories or percentages of 3.3 and 2.8.

This relationship of similarity of association to family protection as a "mutual" phenomenon will be shown further as we move into the succeeding chapters. The relation is the same—that is, it moves in the direction of protection of the families—for all orders of friends and for all cities. It not only protects the A's but the B, C, D, E and F groups.

CONCLUSIONS

This brings out the point that the cumulativity of similarity of backgrounds, points of view and of values of the family-friendship groups is very massive and complicated. Being such it can and does imprint character on the young. It begins with the first friend and goes clear out through the fifth friend of a fifth friend, or through an average of twenty-five layers of human beings. Insofar as this cumulativity of friendship groupings is a help to the family in holding it together as husband-wife and parent-child, the influence is fairly insurmountable. From the inner viewpoint, it may be spoken of as a type of "closed social system." From the outer point of view it is an open social system but only opened through friend-friend families of the same general type as the original family studied.

Thus we reach the conclusion that the interlocking of groups of friend-families makes the small social system of closed friend-families a part of a larger system which is similar to it. The resources of the larger social system are available in some degree to the smaller social system and help it meet many problems which the smaller system by itself could not easily surmount.

The friendship groups and their interlocking connections with similar groups explain how family values have been able to survive and are surviving on a civilization-adequate level under the most complex of modern social conditions. The intimate friends "close" the group about the family but they and their friends "open" it when this is needed or desirable.

How is it possible for families to hold values in the modern city when they are always at arms against the sea of troubles presented by differing values? We may compare a family system to a strong house with doors locked on the outside. Anyone can leave but only those with keys can enter. The parents control the keys. In successful families they share these keys with similarly motivated friend-families but only on durance of good, helpful behavior. These keys of the inner-sanctum cannot be entrusted to those who are unknown. Strangers keep out!

FRIEND GROUPS PREVENT DIVORCE

chapter V HOMER MADE AN OBSERVATION THAT FRIENDSHIP
among good people enabled "the good ones to learn
from each other" and that it "helped the young to avoid error,"
"the old to avoid weakness" and "the strong to (accomplish)
noble deeds." In a sense, this study is a test of these Homeric
views.

In the present chapter, which deals with the influence of
similarity of groupings upon divorce or desertion, we seek to show
that inter-family friendship helps the "old to avoid weakness."
In the next chapter, which deals with friendship and records of
juvenile arrests, we seek to show its influence upon helping the
"young to keep from error." In a very apt way, the influence of
family-friendships upon the motivation of teen-agers to complete
high school courses is a measure of its significance in enabling
"the strong to noble deeds."

FRIENDSHIP GROUPS AND HOMES BROKEN BY DIVORCE

Here a broken home is defined as one reporting a divorce or
desertion. In a later analysis, the concept will be expanded to include homes broken by the death of a spouse.

The study of the relation of family-friendships to divorce or
desertion is presented first in this analysis for several reasons. One
is that family success is a total pattern of behavior, and disruption of the husband-wife relation is generally the first flaw to
appear in the time sequence. That is, divorce and desertions
occur most frequently in families before there are teen-age children. The arrests of teen-agers by police or the failure of the
child to continue his education come later. Evidence exists of a
relation, of a chain reaction type, between divorces and desertions
and juvenile arrests and failure to continue in schools after the
compulsory age limit. The divorce or desertion may be spoken of

as a "cause" of delinquency in the sense that the divorce or desertion precedes the child's acts, and appears to bring about the delinquencies.

DIVORCE FACILITATES LATER JUVENILE TROUBLE

The disruption of the modern Russian family system began about the time of the 1917 Revolution, and soon reached a high peak of easy divorce and "factual" marriage. The reaction against the undisciplined crop of teen-agers coming out of these mass divorces was evident in the family reform law of 1936 and was shown in the practical elimination of divorce by Russian law in the new revised family code of 1944 and 1945.

In our American family the great divorce disruption began among the civilian population in 1942-43 and reached a peak among returned soldiers and civilians alike in 1948. Adding fifteen years to these two dates, juvenile delinquency should now be (and is) very high. Unless the situation changes or something unusual happens, this juvenile rebellion may possibly rise to new peaks from 1959 through 1963. It is entirely possible, and most probable, that our present Senate Commission on Juvenile Delinquency is a popular reflection of the beginning rise to that peak. The public may be sensing a time of juvenile troubles.

While we have a number of books by misinformed persons who claim children do not suffer from divorce, that is not so. It is not a scientific assertion. American, Russian and other experiences indicate that the juvenile crime rate rises markedly among children of divorce when they reach the later teen ages. Also those countries with high divorce rates have high juvenile delinquency. Countries with low divorce rates have much less delinquency. We now have information for nearly every European country and it repeatedly confirms the outlines of this disruptive social pattern.

The present study also shows that good parents and their friends avoid having disrupted families in their intimate circle *even though this disruption is due solely to the death of a parent.* Thus the problem of the broken family has several facets.

In families disrupted by divorce or desertion, we find a "guilt by association" feeling on the part of the child. He feels his father (unlike the majority of fathers) has stained the family by divorcing or deserting or both. No matter what the true reasons for a divorce or desertion, the child ordinarily will not look at the woman left in his home other than as a "blameless mother." Few are the children like those in the Greek tragedy about Orestes and Electra, who conspired together to kill their mother Clytemnestra, in revenge for the killing by her and Aegisthus of their father Agamemnon. It takes a long time for a mother to become a "woman" to her child. In most cases she always remains a mother and never is envisaged in the category of "woman" alone.

The second kind of broken home is when the child or children are born legitimately and of good parents but made quasi-orphans by the death of one of the parents. Here, contrary to what many think, and what we thought at the beginning of this study, a psychosomatic disturbance occurs which may be severe. As shown later, the social network of friends about these quasi-orphaned children is considerably disrupted.

A third kind of broken home, resulting from a death, a desertion or a divorce is that type in which a mother alone, or a mother with the aid of a second husband, has the job of rearing the children. This is an additional shift of pattern within a family after the loss of a father.

QUASI-DESERTION

We asked if there had been a divorce or desertion in the history of each family in this study. We also ascertained whether the present marriage of the mother and of the father was a first or a subsequent one. Thus we know how many of the student and of the friend-families were composed of parents in a first marriage living together with their children. The remaining families included the children living with one or more step-parents, and a few widows with children. The purpose of this part of the study is to find if friendships influenced spousal estrangements, and also if spousal loss by either divorce or death influenced friendship groups.

In explanation it may be said at the beginning that divorce, desertion and the death of a spouse and parent, are very common occurrences in our society. In about nine times out of ten, where there has been a divorce or desertion, the mother is likewise left the custody and most of the support of the children. And generally men, being shorter-lived than women, die first, leaving a widow with children. Additionally, as was pointed out earlier, in 1955 there were seven and a quarter million children, or 12 per cent of all children under 18, living in homes in which one of the parents (or parent and step-parent) were absent. A factor in such situations is what we have called *quasi-desertion*. Absent or divorced husbands refuse to pay alimony to the wife. "Fade-away fathers" can avoid support payments in a society such as ours by moving to another legal jurisdiction. Before the court orders reach them, they move again.

In 1955 public aid to dependent children in the United States included 190,000 families in which the father was currently or previously married to the mother of the children receiving help. Of these 190,000 family cases receiving public help (it did not include desertions or quasi-desertions in which public help was not asked) 47.5 per cent were of fathers who were "plain deserters" without judicial decree, and most of the remainder were "quasi-deserters," having a judicial decree of divorce, annulment or separation, but refusing to support the former wife and children.

In about half the cases of these deserters and quasi-deserters, the absence had been for more than five years. In more than half, the social workers could not find even where the deserters lived.

The same situation is true in other countries with divorce and desertion problems of some magnitude. In 1955 England spent thirty millions of pounds supporting deserted or quasi-deserted children.

The problem of a loss of one or both parents by a death, a divorce or desertion or quasi-desertion not only leaves the woman and children in a difficult situation but also throws much of the total burden of child discipline upon a mother alone. Most cases of juvenile arrests are for teen-age male children. The males in this group are very difficult for a mother alone to handle. They are equally difficult for a step-father to rear properly.

Then again absence of income tends to bring the public as represented by the social worker into the family. The social workers do the best they can in many almost impossible situations. They furnish funds and advise on family matters. Nevertheless they are strangers, and families fear bringing strangers into their intimacy, even though they represent the public interest and are dispensing money.[1]

STEP-PARENTS AND SOCIAL WORKERS

We may summarize broken homes by enumerating the types of cases in which a child is without the direct guidance of both mother and father.

The child lives:

> with mother alone,
> with other relatives,
> with strangers,
> with mother and step-father,
> with father and step-mother,
> with step-father and step-mother.

Each of these classes may be influenced further by lack of money, bringing in social workers to take over the partial support and direction of the child. Each class can arise because of death, divorce, desertion or the incarceration of one or both parents in a prison or a mental hospital. Absence of fathers in the armed forces is a factor.

We do not know how many such at least partially orphaned children there are in the United States but we do know that in 1955 it was considerably more than 12 per cent and probably

---

[1] The reaction of families to social workers is documented in detail in L. V. Koos, *Families in Trouble*, Kings Crown Press, New York, 1946.

nearer 20 per cent, or one out of five of the children under 18 years of age. Our census statistics should tell us about this in detail.

The dispensing of public moneys by social workers, mostly for cases like these, has now reached a point where social workers seem to glorify it as showing the country's humaneness, rather than the failure and defeat of some of its citizens.[2]

The U. S. Census tells us that of every hundred families in 1947, 86 were "husband and wife" families, 2 were families with a head who had never married, and 12 were "broken" families. The trouble with such an analysis as this is that the category "husband and wife" families contains all the remarried widows, widowers, divorced persons and so on. Neither do we know from this just how many of the families were quasi-deserted.

Further, less than half of the "husband and wife" families reported in 1947 had children under 18 years of age in the house. Among broken families, only a third had sons or daughters under 18.

An earlier partial report in the Census of 1940 tried to find the numbers of previous marriages among 650,000 new marriages in twenty-three states. About twenty thousand of the women and an equal number of the men did not answer the question. For those answering it was computed that about 87.4 per cent of the brides and 86.9 per cent of the grooms were making their first marriage.

These scattered statistics reaffirm our above conclusion that about one out of five children lives in a disrupted home of one or the other of the seven classes enumerated.[3]

INFLUENCE OF FRIEND GROUPS UPON DIVORCE
IN STUDENT FAMILIES

Table 21 shows that in every city the parents of the students have a very low divorce or desertion rate when they and their

[2] See Frances Lomas Feldman, *The Family in a Money World,* Family Services Association of America, New York, 1957, Chapters I, II *et passim.*

[3] See *The American Family,* a special publication prepared for the National Conference on Family Life, Washington, May 1948, Chapter I for a resume of the official statistics on broken homes as far as these are known.

Table 21

FRIENDSHIP SIMILARITY AND DIVORCE OR DESERTION AMONG STUDENT PARENTAL FAMILIES

Percentages of Student's Parents Divorced or Deserted by City

Traits in common with friends*	Boston	New Orleans	St. Louis	Denver	Omaha	Los Angeles
None	11.1	3.8	13.1	10.2	11.8	20.7
One only	7.3	6.9	12.9	10.7	9.7	15.3
Two only	4.7	8.0	10.1	9.8	8.8	12.6
Three only	4.6	6.5	7.1	7.4	8.3	12.3
All four	3.5	4.6	5.8	7.2	8.1	12.9
Total	5.4	6.6	9.4	9.3	9.0	14.6

* The traits in common are income class, region of origin of husband, religious confession of wife and kinship.

friends have four traits in common, that they have a higher divorce or desertion rate when they and their friends have fewer common traits. Similarity among good friends is associated with a falling rate.

The parents of high school seniors and their friends are already a selected sample. The broken family rate among student families of the worst type is lower than that of the general population. This statement means this: any given city studied has an average rate of spousal estrangements much higher than among the families producing high school graduates.

In the Long Beach section of Los Angeles, for instance, where the number of divorces granted every year throughout the general population practically equals the number of marriages, the most disintegrated groups of our student families (those with nothing in common with first friend) had divorce and desertion rates of only 25.7 per cent. This dramatizes the fact that high school senior families and their friends are much above the mass of families in avoiding divorce and desertion even though they differ in goodness among themselves.⁴

Hereafter this study's "divorce-desertion percentage" will be called the "divorce rate" because divorce and desertion is a cumbersome bit of terminology. It really is a "disruption of spousal coexistence within the home" because Catholics in particular and some other confessions frown upon divorce and permit only separations at the most. However, the term "spousal disruptions" is also cumbersome.

Now we have to explain the apparent exceptions for New Orleans in the atypical low divorce rates for the families with "none" or "one only" traits in common. This is due to a small sample in this category. We were forced to take here only parochial schools which gives a homogenous sample in a rather homogenous city. Of the thousands of families studied there only 21 had nothing in common with first friend, 34 nothing with second, 30 nothing with third, 34 nothing with fourth, and 41 nothing with fifth. Numbers small as these change remarkably with the addition or subtraction of only one divorce.

RELATION OF FRIENDSHIP TO DIVORCE AMONG THE
"OTHER" FAMILIES

Table 22 shows the relation of friendship similarity to divorce, not among the student families, but among their family friends. The same pattern follows in every city as was found for the student families with similar friends.

Here the anomalous situation discussed a paragraph back about New Orleans straightens itself out because since each student family reported upon about five friends, our numbers in the computation are greater. Thus in New Orleans a quarter, or one in four, of the friend-families with nothing in common with the student families were divorced or deserted. This contrasts with only 3 per cent among those friend-families with all four

---

⁴ Estimating proportions divorced in a population from a given years' ratio of divorces to marriages is very treacherous, but we are sure the above statement is true.

Table 22

FRIENDSHIP SIMILARITY AND DIVORCE OR DESERTION
AMONG THE PARENT FRIEND FAMILIES

Percentages of Friend Families Divorced or Deserted by City

Traits in common with students' parents*	Boston	New Orleans	St. Louis	Denver	Omaha	Los Angeles
None	24.5	25.0	24.2	14.3	24.1	15.6
One only	7.6	8.7	11.6	9.2	12.7	10.9
Two only	5.1	4.8	7.2	6.9	4.3	8.3
Three only	3.9	3.7	4.4	5.7	3.5	7.5
All four	2.6	3.0	3.6	4.3	4.5	5.2
Total	6.0	5.3	7.9	7.8	7.5	10.0

* The traits in common are income class, region of origin of husband, religious confession of wife, and kinship.

traits in common with the student families.

This analysis brings out a point alluded to in the previous chapters, and this is that the social organization of friend-families is built on the same principles. This, in turn, takes us back to the opening lines of Tolstoi's *Anna Karenina* in which the author remarked that in essence "all good families are alike." [5]

Since the friend-families are good families, too, they have other friends (which we did not study and which are different from the student families). Out of their continued association with these good families, of which the student family is only one, they likewise gained a protection against divorce.

ST. LOUIS SHOWS THAT SIMILAR FRIEND GROUPS PREVENT SPOUSAL TROUBLES

In order to demonstrate this relation in detail we give the full data (Tables 23 and 24) for St. Louis, Mo. Here on account of its

[5] "Happy families are all alike; every unhappy family is unhappy in its own way." Part I, Chapter I, opening lines.

Table 23

FRIENDSHIP SIMILARITY AND DIVORCE OR DESERTION
AMONG STUDENT FAMILIES

(Friends are ranked in closeness from one through five)

(Illustrative Data for St. Louis, Mo.)

*Percentages Divorced Among Student Families According
to Similarity with Friend-Families*

Number of common traits with friends*	First friend	Second friend	Third friend	Fourth friend	Fifth friend
None	19.5	14.2	12.7	9.8	13.3
One only	13.1	12.6	14.1	13.4	11.3
Two only	11.5	10.4	10.3	9.1	9.0
Three only	7.1	7.2	7.2	7.2	6.3
All four	6.3	6.8	4.4	4.8	5.7

* The traits in common are income class, region of origin of husband, religious confession of wife, and kinship.

size and the complete coverage of our sample, we have large numbers—2,526 student families and 12,630 friend-families. These tables show that divorced and deserted families are kept at great social distance from the student families. In addition they also show the general and striking lower rates for divorce or desertion among families whose friendships are similar.

We may elaborate this as follows: If there were no relation between similarity of friendship and spousal estrangement, each pocket in Table 23 would have an average of about 9.4 per cent of divorce or desertion reported for it. Instead the table begins with 19.4 per cent of divorce or desertion among student families with nothing in common with their first friend and drops to 6.3 per cent among those who have four traits in common with the first friend. The relationship goes down as one moves across the table in any direction from "none" in common with friend one to "four" in common with friend five.

Table 24, which gives divorces or desertions among the friend-families of students' parents in St. Louis, shows the same relations as Table 23 except that it is complementary. It shows divorce rates among the friend-families according to their similarities with student families. If similarity of friendship surroundings were not a factor in reduced spousal breakups, every pocket in Table 24 should have about 7.9 per cent divorces in it. Instead it exactly resembles Table 23. Friend *one* has 20.4 per cent of divorces and desertions when nothing is held in common with student family number one, but falls to 3.3 per cent when all things are in common with the first friend. But moving across the page for each row, the proportions of divorce and desertion rise.

Table 24

FRIENDSHIP SIMILARITY AND DIVORCE OR DESERTION AMONG FRIEND-FAMILIES

(Friends are ranked in closeness from one through five)

(Illustrative Data for St. Louis, Mo.)

Percentages Divorced or Deserted Among Friend-Families According to Similarity with Student Families

Number of common traits with student families*	First friend	Second friend	Third friend	Fourth friend	Fifth friend
None	20.4	17.2	27.7	20.2	33.1
One only	9.5	9.9	10.7	15.4	12.8
Two only	4.8	6.4	9.2	8.5	7.2
Three only	3.3	4.4	4.9	3.8	6.1
All four	3.3	2.9	5.9	2.4	3.2

* The traits in common are income class, region of origin of husband, religious confession of wife and kinship. All cities show these identical relations by rank of friend and similarity with friends but there are slight irregularities due to smallness of sizes of numbers involved. St. Louis is an average of our cities and with reports on 12,630 families gives only five pockets with less than four hundred families for rates.

DIFFERENCES BETWEEN FIRST AND FIFTH FAMILIES BY CITY
SHOWS THAT SIMILAR FRIENDS PREVENT BREAKING

In order to establish the generality of our association we
present in Tables 25 and 26 the relations for six cities between

Table 25

STUDENT FAMILY DIVORCE OR DESERTION RATES ACCORDING
TO SIMILARITY WITH FIRST FRIEND ONLY

(*Proportions Divorced or Deserted in Student Families*)

Traits in common with first friend*	Boston	New Orleans	St. Louis	Denver	Omaha	Los Angeles
None	13.5	4.8	19.5	10.1	14.1	25.2
One only	9.8	4.4	13.1	11.9	10.0	16.4
Two only	4.9	8.7	11.5	10.0	8.8	14.8
Three only	5.3	6.1	7.1	7.9	10.4	9.3
All four	2.0	5.6	6.3	8.6	10.5	12.7

* The traits in common are income class, region of origin of husband,
religious confession of wife and kinship.

Table 26

STUDENT FAMILY DIVORCE OR DESERTION RATES ACCORDING
TO SIMILARITY WITH FIFTH FRIEND ONLY

(*Proportions Divorced or Deserted in Student Families*)

Traits in common with fifth friend*	Boston	New Orleans	St. Louis	Denver	Omaha	Los Angeles
None	8.6	7.3	13.3	9.7	13.9	19.7
One only	4.0	8.2	11.3	10.7	9.3	11.9
Two only	4.6	8.3	9.0	11.1	9.0	11.3
Three only	4.7	5.6	6.3	4.6	3.4	12.6
All four	4.3	4.9	5.7	2.9	5.8	14.6

* The traits in common are income class, region of origin of husband,
religious confession of wife and kinship. The religious confession of the
husbands was used in Los Angeles.

similarity of family friendships and the divorce and desertion rates for first and fifth friends. We will not discuss now the results in detail except to note their common traits. These are the universality of the influence of friendship upon divorce by city, and universality for each city by first and by fifth friend. (This relationship is also true for family *two,* family *three* and family *four* and for the friend-families.)

Thus in every city, with only minor variations, social groups of friends reduce the divorce rates among the student families and their friend-families. The more the friends are similar, the greater is the reduction in divorce and desertion.

THIS IS A NEW DISCOVERY

We prove this in detail for the sixty thousand families studied because it is something new in sociology, something important and something every family trying to become successful can emulate. We have indicated earlier, and will point out again, that this "something new" is the invention of American families themselves. We do not know whether it was invented consciously or unconsciously. Our cities, however, are so newly organized and heterogenous that we believe it could not have come about by example, but must be a discovery or rediscovery.

We call it a "discovery" because the former rural backgrounds of the American urban population have been fixed and static over generations and centuries. In these rural backgrounds social relations were disturbed only by epidemics and wars. Consequently the individual grew up, in a moulded social situation, with his place fixed in his family and his family's place fixed in the community. Strangers were few and far between so that they became an event in the village.

All at once, as a result of migration to the cities, all this "fixity of social relations" was broken up. New friends had to be found and tested. Migration and the making of new "mutual aid and comfort groups," or psychological supports, is an experience of a type and scale not hitherto faced by American families for many generations.

SIMILAR GOOD FRIENDS ARE A "CAUSE" OF LOWER DIVORCES

Our problem now is to analyze how this relation between similar family friends and lowered divorce rates works. We want to know whether or not it is a "causal" relation. Any association and especially this one *may* exist without causal significance because good families may simply choose to live together. It may be argued that they *were* good and did not become good because they associated together.[6]

Our own conclusion is that the families sought lowered divorce rates and therefore associated with other families of similar good ideals. Unity and stability in husband-wife relations is a creative act based upon intention, and a social environment which reinforces this intention is a step towards its attainment. Most persons enter marriage with an intention to make it permanent. The familiar statement "till death do us part" is an epitomization of that intention to establish a permanent and stable marriage union of husband and wife.

When we examine the negative cases, or those thousands of newly married families not shortly put into a social environment which reinforces this original marriage intention, we note that these are the very situations where the extremely high divorce, desertion and disruption rates exist.

WAR MARRIAGE SEPARATIONS PROVE THIS

Take, for instance, the war marriages, or those consummated shortly before the male enters the armed services during wars. Here artificial conditions interfere with the reinforcing of the intention. A few years later the male returns from the service. Both of the personalities of the husband and wife have changed in the meantime but not in a similar environment.

These classes of war-separated persons have been prone to high rates of marital disruptions in all countries, in all wars and

---

[6] We realize the dangers and logical problems of the attribution of cause to coexistence of variables but, in addition to coexistence, our conclusion is based upon logical necessity.

in all times both past and present.[7] A few statistics for the beginning and end of World War II will illustrate this.

Table 27

DIVORCES IN 1940 & 1946 PER 1000 MARRIAGES

Country	1940 (*beginning of war*)	1946 (*end of war*)
United States	212	400
Canada	31	73
England & Wales	22	81
France	46	207
Belgium	28	98
Netherlands	46	148
Denmark	108	212
Norway	46	80
Australia	61	106
New Zealand	83	148

All these were mobilized countries. Divorces went up in other countries nearby during this period but not nearly so drastically. In all these mobilized countries, divorces doubled, tripled or quadrupled between 1940 and 1946.

PROOFS FROM URBANIZATION OF CUSTOM-MARRIED PERSONS

A second outstanding negative case is illustrated by the broken marriages in numerous Latin American countries. In many of these there are two cultures with different marriage systems, the Western and the native or Indian. Indians (Aztecs, Toltecs, Mayan in Mexico) marry with good intentions under one system, the village or customary one, and then migrate to cities

---

[7] This was recognized in Roman history. In the reorganization of Roman family law in the Novella code (535-550 A. D.) divorce practices were reorganized. Divorces on account of long war-separations were called *bona gratia* (excusable) as opposed to others in which the guilty party (defendant) might be penalized in several ways.

where they are put under another system and the social environment, with its older sanctions, is removed.

Once these "village-custom" newly married people are in these large cities and dispersed among the civil married populations, they are outside and away from village sanctions which formerly would have preserved the households. High rates of desertion are prevalent. Many men simply move off on the spur of the moment and take another wife and have another brood of children. Nothing seems able to prevent this. They are then not legally married according to Mexican civil law or church ceremony. Friends, kinsmen and village neighbors who would ordinarily try to hold a marriage together are absent. As a result the problems of child legitimacy and of responsibility for support of wives and the proper upbringing of children are very great.[8] The social security administration in Mexico is now endeavoring to bring these people under civil marriage by mass propaganda. Great marriage ceremonies are performed for persons already living together and, in many cases, with several children.

In the summer of 1957, mass marriages of twenty-six thousand couples were consummated in Mexican cities. The largest was of 4,007 couples in Mexico City on Sunday, August 4, 1957. The wedding had previously been set for the preceding Sunday, July 28, but it was delayed for one week by a heavy earthquake. Here the Social Security Administration of Mexico is trying to use certain legal sanctions which, in the absence of others, will help hold these families together. The sanctions are social security rights and benefits.

---

[8] On this problem see *The Legal Position of the Illegitimate Child*, League of Nations, Geneva, IV 6 Social Questions, 1939. In the Latin American countries at this time very high roles for illegitimacy were reported but these were spurious because only civil or church-civil marriage was considered as legitimate. At that time urbanization had not gained great grounds in Latin America. Now it has. See T. Lynn Smith, *Current Social Trends and Problems in Latin America*, University of Florida Press, Gainesville, Florida, 1957, pp. 2 ff.

PROOFS FROM SOCIOLOGICAL THEORY

In addition to these negative proofs, in which it is shown that the absence of reinforcing environmental groups is associated with extremely high rates for divorce and other disruptions, there are positive findings of importance.

One of the commonest truisms in social behavior is the correlation between groups and ideals or aims. Familiar illustrations are armies for wars, priesthoods for religious purposes, corporations for economic gains and other associations to eliminate given diseases or for the study of various sciences.

Human life does not go in a helter-skelter manner nor has it achieved its present level by accident. Every stage, every development, every aim, has been fomented by a given type of social organization. These organizations vary according to what is needed to achieve the aims for which they were formed.

All these organizations unconsciously and unpredictably influence their members. Durkheim showed this in his study of *Suicide*.[9]

People do not get married and have children ordinarily to avoid a high risk of suicide. Neither do they join orthodox religions for that purpose. However, those that do have a very much lower rate for suicide.

We will not elaborate this positive aspect of the proof that forms of social organization have deep influences on human character and behavior, because it is the fundamental tenet of good sociology. We simply indicate it as one of the reasons why we think the selection of close similar friends has a decided causal influence upon the numbers of divorces and desertions (as well as other family troubles) in those groups.

CONCLUSIONS

These reasons why friendship similarity protects against divorce or desertion will later be further elaborated. However,

---

[9] A translation of this classic was published by Free Press in 1951. See especially Section III of the work, pp. 297 *ff.*

several things deserve stressing. First of all, we have so many reports of lower divorces and desertions in similar friend groups from so many different cities that we are sure we have something of great importance.

Our starting problem was to find why some children finished high schools in these cities when more, admittedly equally capable, did not do so. As later chapters show, we are attributing it to the capacity and ability of parents to control the value environments of their children. In doing this job of social control, they have found the admission of similar intimate friends to their homes a key device. Our analysis also shows that the family-friend form of social organization likewise promotes a greater ability in parents to get along in harmony with each other. In the next chapter we will show it reflected in lower rates of juvenile arrest.

One elusive phase of the problem is whether these social advantages result from "creativity by the parents" or are merely accidents accruing to happy people. Were they merely inadvertently being successful with their children? In general our analysis, as already started and as will be elaborated later, shows that a successful family is a conscious parental creativity, a choice of a type of life. Somehow, somewhere these parents got the idea that if things were done this way the results would be good, so they did it, and achieved the results. In other words we believe that successful family living is primarily a result of voluntarism and causality, not of happenstance or cultural determinism. In many respects the building of a protective shell of similar family friends is a "new" social discovery.

FRIEND GROUPS PREVENT JUVENILE ARRESTS

chapter VI   JUVENILE ARRESTS CONCERN MAINLY MALES AMONG
the teen-agers. Since divorce comes in most cases
before the time the male children are teen-agers, then we have
to consider the divorce or its prevention a primary action. We
believe the circle of intimate similar friends about the house is
directly related to the parent's ability to keep their children from
conduct leading to arrest.[1] We also find that this ability to control
the children is achieved in a considerable degree by a substitution
of behavior. That is, the children are encouraged to do well and
to continue in schools as a substitute for behavior which might
get them into trouble.

The reasons for this will be discussed in detail later. Right
now we point out that the circles of friends—the living ramparts
which keep harmony in the home, and help avoid divorce and
desertion—also make a foundation from which the later "social"
control of children is erected.

Logically it follows that good friends help make good parents,
and good parents make good children. We not only think this is
true but we also believe that the circles of values about the homes
made by these friends also influence the children directly. However, before continuing this argument, let us present the relationships between similar friend-families and the arrest rates for
children in these families.

Each student answered this simple question for his own and
his friend-families: *Has any child in this family been arrested for
delinquency at any time?* Yes. . . . No. . . . . The questionnaires
were anonymous, let us repeat, given in classrooms under close

---

[1] See Paul H. Jacobson, "Differentials of Divorce by Duration of
Marriages and Size of Family," *American Sociological Review,* 15, (1950)
243 *et passim.*

supervision of teachers and with little time to reflect upon the possibility of duplicity or the meaning of the answers.

Table 28

FAMILIES REPORTING ONE OR MORE
ARRESTS OF A JUVENILE

Percentages

City	Student families	Friend-families
Boston	6	5
New Orleans	2	2
St. Louis	8	7
Denver	9	7
Omaha	12	7
Los Angeles	15	8

Arrest records (Table 28) among the student families ranged from 6 per cent in Boston to 15 per cent in Long Beach. Among the friend-families of the students' parents, arrest records ranged from 5 per cent in Boston to 8 per cent in Long Beach. We believe the unusually low arrest figures for New Orleans are an anomaly because of a selected orthodox group, which had lower rates than the average.

In general, friend-families had lower arrest records than student families because, it appears both arrest-record and non-arrest-record parent families try to avoid arrest-record friend-families. The student families were chosen automatically by taking *all* in the high school senior classes. But the student families had chosen their own friends, and been selective.

CITIES WITH MORE ARRESTS SHOW GREATER AVOIDANCE
OF ARREST-HISTORY FAMILIES

Also, the "polarization," or separation into opposing classes, of families with and without records of child arrests was greater for the newer cities, where the problem was more prevalent and critical. Among the Boston student families 6 per cent reported arrests and had 5 per cent among the friends. In St. Louis the rate among student families was 8 per cent and among friends 7 per cent. But in Omaha the arrest rates were 12 per cent among student families and only 7 per cent among friends. In Los Angeles the rate was 15 per cent among student families and only 8 per cent among friends.

It should be made clear that throughout this study such figures are *not* for juvenile delinquency and should never be so reported. Delinquency is a chronic status, marked off by a court action and a finding of guilt. Almost any boy can get in trouble with the local police once or twice. According to our Senate Commission on Juvenile Delinquency, at least two of every three children who are arrested are remanded to their parents for *family action only,* and no public record is made of the arrest nor does it come before the courts. In these two out of three cases, the family action eventually corrects the juvenile misbehavior and the children do not become delinquents.

However, although ours are not figures on bona-fide juvenile delinquency, they concern a like kind of behavior. Hence, an analysis of controls of arrest records by the good families would apply generally to the basic control of juvenile delinquency.

Every family is vulnerable to juvenile troubles, but most surmount them. We see this in an analysis of figures on juvenile arrest histories. Some of the most pertinent results may be summarized here.

THE POOR HAVE THE HIGHEST JUVENILE-ARREST PATTERNS

Low-income families in all cities have much higher arrest rates than the good families we studied. Part of this is due to the fact that low-income families live in sections of the city where room is lacking for the normal activity of restless teen-agers and the police are close to the door step. The mothers in low-income families are more often employed outside of the home and consequently are unable to exert full parental control.[2] Also, however,

---

[2] A definitive study "Working Mothers and Delinquency" by Sheldon and Eleanor Glueck, *Mental Hygiene,* July, 1957, shows that outside employment by mothers is important and "causally" related to delinquency.

part of this low-income relation with juvenile arrest records is due to the high incidence of broken families in the juvenile-arrest groups.

The death of a spouse is a factor in a lower income for the family, and also in outside work, and inadequate supervision of children, by mothers. Persons remarried "for any cause" in the United States, as shown by the Census analysis by Paul C. Glick, have less income on the average than similarly employed individuals who are not remarried. If after twelve-fifteen years of marriage, an American worker enumerated in the 1946 sample census was living with a second or subsequent wife, he was making $300 less than one living with a first wife.

Among the families we have studied, the relation of first marriages to juvenile arrests is shown in Table 29.

Table 29

REMARRIAGES AND ARREST RECORDS OF CHILDREN

City	Proportions of "all" families studied which were first marriages	Proportions of arrest-record families studied which were first marriages	Difference in percentages of arrest-record families
Boston	88	69	19
New Orleans	88	59	29
St. Louis	82	54	28
Denver	86	66	20
Omaha	84	60	24

JUVENILE-ARREST PATTERNS IN WELL-TO-DO FAMILIES

The low-income families have a much higher proportion of juvenile arrest records than the total population of good families studied. But the proportion is also higher, if only slightly so, among the upper-income families. Apparently families with incomes of more than $10,000 a year had more than average difficulty in controlling their children. Even though, with their superior economic status, they probably have more to give their children, and hence keep them away from the streets. They also have more "connections" by which to compose without arrests, or by the quashing of arrests, the brushes between their children and the police.

We previously noted a tendency in some cities for the children of the wealthy to get into trouble simply because they had too much freedom and economic goods (spending money, automobiles, etc.). Among these is Boston. A teen-ager with ready access to a powerful automobile is very liable to get into trouble with police—and not only for illegal parking.

Sample figures from our study for "all" families, as compared with juvenile-arrest-record families in the below $2,000 and above $10,000 brackets are:

In Boston, 5 per cent of all families were under $2,000 in income but had a delinquent-arrest rate of 18.7 per cent. Families above $10,000 were 12.6 per cent of the total, with a delinquent-arrest rate of 14.9 per cent. In Denver, in Omaha and in New Orleans both the poor and the well-to-do had higher rates for juvenile arrests than their proportions of all totals. In each of these cities (Boston, Denver, Omaha and New Orleans), the middle-income groups had by far the lowest arrest-record rate.

St. Louis was a partial exception in that the wealthy did not have a disproportionate percentage of the arrest records. While the poor consituted 9 per cent of the total, and provided 20 per cent of the arrest families, the wealthy, constituting 15 per cent of the total families, had exactly the same (15%) arrest rate. The middle-group families, from $2,000 to less than $10,000, constituted 76 per cent of all families, but with an arrest rate of 65 per cent.

For reasons inherent in earlier tabulation difficulties we did not make the income versus arrest-record tabulation for Los Angeles.

THE BROKEN HOME AND THE TEEN-AGER

The influence of "poverty" and "too much money" in relation to arrest records are well suspected facts. But they have been overemphasized as "causal relations" during this last century of "class warfare" propaganda. The Marxians have played them up to emphasize their claims of the "degradation" of the poor and the "dissoluteness" of the wealthy.

The greatest patterns of juvenile arrest appear to occur mostly, in a causal sense, in broken homes: Those of desertion or divorce and of widowhood. In such cases, according to our American practice, the woman alone is left with growing children. Males die earlier than females and widows are much more frequent than widowers. The woman alone, when she has children, seems not as able to cope with their supervision and control.

The divorcee or widow remarries if she can. This means several things to the family. A shock, or "pattern of family disharmony," seems to influence the children and they take it seriously during their teen-age periods. The families of this type are avoided by families not having had this experience. We find this in detail for all cities and all orders of friends. Where the problem is most prevalent, as in the newer cities, the avoidance is most striking.

Most juvenile arrests are of male teen-agers. These are the ones least susceptible to control by mothers. Step-fathers also seem to have great difficulty with them. With the female teen-ager, juvenile delinquency generally is concerned with sexual activities, and the severe penalties for criminal conversation, rape, statutory rape, violation of "age of consent" and pre-marital pregnancy form a deterrent to both for the teen-ager and the other person or persons involved. Girls are guarded more carefully by families and by the public than boys.

In various cities the proportions of broken homes among the group reporting juvenile arrests were from four to seven times greater than the average among all families.

Some sample rates for homes in which both parents have had a former marriage: In Boston all families had only a 3.64 per cent rate for such homes, but arrest-record families had a 15.45 per cent rate—an increase of more than four times.

In New Orleans "total broken homes" increased the arrest

rate by 548 per cent. In St. Louis the increase was 496 per cei
In Denver the increase was 217 per cent. In Omaha the increa
was 347 per cent.

These families are "good" ones. Whatever mistakes they ha
made, they have in nearly all cases been able to recuperate. (
needs to be remembered that juvenile-arrest patterns—the st
toward delinquency—are a very complicated matter.)

While it is apparent that wealth and poverty create conditio
of particular hazard in successful child control, the devastati
influences upon the children are when families are broken. Th
the real influences leading to juvenile arrests are set in motio

THE STEP-PARENT HAS MORE DIFFICULTY THAN PARENTS

Further proof of this was brought out in the analysis of r
marriages in which differentiation was made among a first or
subsequent marriage for the mother or father or both. When
mother makes a subsequent marriage to an unmarried man, s
brings with her children by her first marriage. These are rais
in a household which consists of a mother, a step-father a
possible half-brothers and sisters. The widows, divorcees, ste
mothers or step-fathers do the best they can, but apparently re
parents are more successful in guiding teen-age males th
mothers alone or step-fathers in combination with real mothe
As was said earlier, a subsequent married father, and especia
if he and his new wife have children afterwards, returns us ge
erally to the household of mother and father, parents and ch
dren. That is, the father tends to hide or to play down his pre
ous marital failure.

We are not condemning about these forms of behavior, b
trying to explain the results of our study. We are absolutely su
as to the generality and universality of the above claims in all t
cities and situations which we investigated.

FRIEND SIMILARITY AND JUVENILE ARREST

Before we go further in this analysis we now have to refer
two tables, 30 and 31, which compare similarity of friends a

juvenile-arrest records. These parallel the tables given in the last chapter, comparing similarity of friends and divorce or desertion records.

Table 30

FRIENDSHIP SIMILARITY AND JUVENILE ARREST RECORDS AMONG STUDENTS' PARENTAL FAMILIES

Percentages of Student Families Reporting One Arrest or More

Traits in common with friends*	Boston	New Orleans	St. Louis	Denver	Omaha	Los Angeles
None	8.1	1.9	11.6	10.2	16.4	14.9
One only	4.9	2.2	9.2	8.9	14.5	14.3
Two only	5.9	2.6	8.0	8.1	11.7	12.7
Three only	4.6	2.5	7.5	7.3	10.0	12.2
All four	4.4	2.0	7.6	8.0	9.2	16.9
Total average for city	5.3	2.4	8.2	8.3	12.0	13.7

*The traits in common are income class, region of origin of husband, religious confession of wife and kinship.

Table 30 takes up each city and shows how the rate for juvenile arrest varies among "pockets of friends" from those with no traits in common to those with all four traits (economics, region of origin, religion and kindred) in common.

Table 31 shows the rates among friend-families. In Boston, for instance, 298 student families associated with 298 friend-families with whom they had none of these traits in common. Table 30 shows that these 298 student families had arrest rates of 8.1 per cent, and Table 31 that the 298 friend-families had 21.5 per cent. At the bottom of the column for Boston, you will see that 573 student families associated with 573 friend-families with whom they had all four traits in common. The 573 student families had a 4.4 per cent arrest rate, and the 573 friend-families, 1.7 per cent.

Table 31

FRIENDSHIP SIMILARITY AND JUVENILE ARREST RECORDS AMONG PARENTAL FRIEND-FAMILIES

Families Reporting One Arrest or More

Traits in common with students' parents*	Boston	New Orleans	St. Louis	Denver	Omaha	Los Angel
None	21.5	18.8	20.1	14.0	19.7	13.4
One only	7.2	4.1	8.9	8.7	9.5	8.4
Two only	3.9	2.2	5.3	4.4	5.7	6.5
Three only	3.1	2.3	3.6	4.7	3.9	4.9
All four	1.7	1.6	2.9	4.9	4.2	4.4
Total average for city	5.0	3.0	6.2	6.6	7.0	7.8

*The traits in common are income class, region of origin of husban religious confession of wife and kinship.

Our St. Louis data were similar. As seen in Table 32 frier *one* group, with nothing in common with parents, had 15 per ce of arrests but friend *one* with four things in common had on 2.8 per cent; friend *two* similarly 13.4 per cent and 2.4 per cen friend *three* 20.5 per cent and 2.6 per cent; friend *four* 19.1 per cent and 2.9 per cent; friend *five* 29.5 per cent and 5.1 per cen

No matter how one may explain it, "good families" that a successful in controlling their teen-age males—the prospectiv source of juvenile delinquents—seem to keep "bad families" far distant from their households as possible. In place of "ba families" (those with an arrest record) they substitute famili "like themselves" which are "good." This use of "good" famili as intimate friends, they apparently believe, serves to help preve a first and subsequent juvenile arrests and hence deters juveni delinquency.

Table 32

FRIEND SIMILARITY AND JUVENILE ARREST RECORDS
AMONG FRIEND-FAMILIES

(Friends are ranked in closeness from one through five)

(Illustrative Data for St. Louis, Mo.)

*Percentages of Arrest Records Among Friend-Families
According To Similarity With Friend-Families*

Number of common traits with student families*	First friend	Second friend	Third friend	Fourth friend	Fifth friend
None	15.0	13.4	20.5	19.1	29.5
One only	6.6	9.4	9.7	11.1	7.9
Two only	4.6	6.3	5.4	4.6	5.9
Three only	2.3	2.8	4.9	5.5	3.8
All four	2.8	2.4	2.6	2.9	5.1
Average	4.3	5.6	6.8	7.4	7.8

* The similarities are measured by income class, region of origin of husband, religious confession of wife and kinship. All cities show these identical relations by rank of friends and similarity with friends but there are slight irregularities due to smallness of sizes of number involved. St. Louis is an average of our cities and with reports on 15,000 families gives only five pockets with less than four hundred families for the rates.

THE UNITY OF AIM IN SUCCESSFUL FAMILIES

Before we make any further remarks about these four tables on juvenile delinquency and type of family friendship, it will be helpful if we reappraise the situation. Our main problem is to find how some families in large cities, and increasingly greater numbers of them, keep their teen-agers in high school. Juvenile delinquency, divorce, desertion and other matters are side issues. If we incidentally find something new about any of these matters, it is an extra gain and must not detract from the main issue of the study.

Our hypothesis is this. A healthy family tries to gain all its three main objectives, keeping parents together, rearing children properly (keeping them out of the hands of the police) and giving them the standard current-and-accepted best goals in life. They seek to combine "good" husband-wife, "good" parent-child and "good" family-cultural relations.

In a large degree, the methods for accomplishing each ought to be about the same because they are all attempts by a social organization—the family—to secure for its members conformity, success, continuity and happiness.

If the methods of this social organization to secure one of the three particular goals, (marriage harmony, child rearing or goal implantation), are different from the methods used for the others, then at least they must not be antithetical. If the methods used in avoiding divorce and juvenile arrest are not the same as those needed for goal implantation in teen-agers, then they must at least not hinder the children in continuing through high school.

But, our study shows conclusively that the three—avoiding divorce, avoiding arrest and avoiding high-school-dropping out— are interrelated matters achieved in general by the same social principles—good home, good neighborhood social surroundings, good ideals or goals and "good" friends.

However, our basic hypothesis goes farther than this. If we can show clearly that avoiding divorce and parent-child estrangement (arrest), not only for the student but also for similar families intimate with them, are achieved by about the same broad methods of social organization, then we have reason to believe that this is a "good" family principle, and may consider it as casting light upon goal implantation within the children.

It must be remembered that our study includes large numbers of the latest arrivals to the United States. These immigrants who came to the United States after 1890 are located in the centers of large cities. Here the chances of upholding the American "credo" of upward mobility and increasing success are most difficult. If these people, mostly without backgrounds of "old Americanism," do this under stress, we feel that their major methods of doing so will be evident in an analysis of the family life.

CONTINUING EDUCATION IS A POSITIVE RESULT OF AVOIDING
DIVORCE AND DELINQUENCY

Each of the goals of the family—parental, child and motivation—are essentially phases of the control of values of members.
The values of husband and wife are controlled by maintaining
the permanency of the marriage vow. The values of the teen-
agers are controlled by preventing them from staining the family
—and themselves—by juvenile acts which lead to arrest. The
values of the young must be shaped into "motives" in order for
them to continue in school. They must substitute schooling for
delinquent-tinged behavior. No child lives in a static condition.

A society at any time has "general directives" which it tries
to give to parents as proposed "musts" or "ideals" in the interests
of the children. Legitimate marriage with its direct parent-child
relation is a "must" both in the written and unwritten laws for the
proper rearing of children; for written laws, our voluminous
family code is proof. Compulsory school attendance up to sixteen
years of age is generally a must; most states do not grant work
permits except for after school hours.

In the same way, the secondary and college education of the
young is now becoming a "must" in a highly technical civilization
such as ours. One can scarcely listen to the radio, look at the
television or read the papers and magazines without being re-
minded constantly on this matter as a "duty." We hear that
"nurses, doctors, teachers, scientists, engineers, are going to be
needed more and more." This message is constantly being emphasized to the audience of adult listeners. After the first Russian
earth satellite these directives on education mounted in a
crescendo.

We are trying to find how the adults translate these "musts"
and "aims" as "motives" into the minds of their teen-agers.
Studies of teen-agers and adolescent youth show that their problems of reaching consistent aims are highly involved. Mature in
body and immature in mentality, youngsters are difficult. And
the problem is further complicated by the fact that only one or a
few mistakes are allowed. Once a child stops school, then, in

most cases, he never returns. When he "knows better," he is tc old.

The question of how to keep the qualified youth in school the question of how to keep a culture dynamic and a civilizatic alive. This is a basic problem of sociology—if not *the* basic on▶ We know that the main differences between groups of peop are "cultural" and that culture is connected with the growth ◀ change of motives from one generation to the next. Once a cultu reaches a given level, and its changes call for new personali▶ types, how does that culture inspire its young to be creative in sense that the parents were not? That is a broad theoretic problem of such a civilization as ours and that is the proble▶ we are seeking to analyze here.

GOOD FAMILY AVOIDANCE OF JUVENILE ARREST-RECORD FAMILI▶

In every city and in every order of friendship in every ci▶ we have the constant fact that *similar friends have much low▶ rates for juvenile arrest than friends with less in common.* Th▶ relationship between similarity of friend groupings and low juv▶ nile-arrest records is true not only for the student families b▶ also friend-families as well. We may illustrate this by rates f▶ the first friend-family in Omaha as given in Table 33.

Table 33

ARREST RECORDS OF STUDENT AND FIRST-FRIEND-FAMILIES
IN OMAHA
(According to Similarities of Friend Groupings)

Traits in common*	Number of families involved		Percentages of familie with arrest records	
	Student families	First-friend-families	Student family	First-frie▶ family
None	99	99	19.2	10.1
One only	229	229	14.8	6.1
Two only	466	466	11.8	5.4
Three only	462	462	11.0	3.9
All four	172	172	8.1	4.1

* These are income, region of origin, religion and kindred.

SIMILAR FRIENDS SURROUND GOOD FAMILIES
AND HELP PRESERVE THEM

The data in Table 33 apply to every city studied and for every order of friend. In Omaha, 99 families had nothing in common with their first friends. (This means that there were 99 pairs of families [99 student families and 99 first-friend-families] who were not kindred, not of the same religious confession, not of the same regional origin and not in the same income grouping.) Of the 99 families of student parents, 19 had a record of at least one juvenile arrest in their family history. Of the 99 friends, 10 had a record of juvenile arrest.

At the other extreme, there were 172 pairs of families (172 parental ones and 172 of their best friends). Each of these 172 pairs had the four measured traits in common. The 172 student families had 14 arrest histories and the 172 friends had 7 arrest histories.

Here is the result! *No matter what circumstance (biological, physical, environmental or social) makes children run afoul of the law, good, similar, intimate friend-families around the home, deter it, prevent it, and help it from getting out of hand. At the same time these friends help to keep the children more interested in life achievement through the school system and make for better husband-wife relations within the home.* These two italicized sentences of 66 words, 9 commas, 2 parentheses, one hyphen, and two periods put the main practical results of our study in a nutshell.

THE FEW BAD-RECORD FAMILIES ARE FAR-AWAY FRIENDS

The second principle of importance is that families try to eliminate friends with arrest records from the social core around them. If they associate with such families at all, they push them into the ranks of *far-away* friends. Most intimate friends have fewer arrest records than the other friends. Here are some figures on arrest rates for friends according to their nearness to student families.

Table 34

ARREST RECORDS FOR FRIENDS
BY NEARNESS TO STUDENT FAMILIES BY CITY

Proportions of Friends with Arrest-Records by Nearness or Rank

City	First friend	Second friend	Third friend	Fourth friend	Fifth friend
Boston	3.4	4.7	4.2	6.3	6.6
New Orleans	1.7	2.4	3.1	3.5	4.4
St. Louis	4.3	5.6	6.8	7.4	7.8
Denver	5.4	6.0	6.9	7.5	7.8
Omaha	5.2	6.5	7.3	8.0	9.5
Los Angeles	7.4	9.0	10.8	11.3	12.4

The third tendency, as noted earlier, is for families to be more careful in picking any arrest-record friends in those cities and those areas where juvenile arrests are most frequent and most a problem. This is a phase of the "greater polarization" between "good" and "bad" families constantly brought up throughout this study.

CONCLUDING REMARKS

In this chapter we grapple with the main problem of our study, the ability of parents to control and to influence the conduct of their teen-age children. Motivating them to keep out of trouble amounts to motivating them to do good things, because no one lives in a vacuum. If they are motivated not to do one thing, then they must be motivated to do a substitute thing.

If keeping youths out of trouble is achieved by use of these selective friends, it is also the factor which induces them to finish their education. Schooling is substituted for troublesome activities. Successful parents do not say to a child: "Stay home tonight." Rather they say: "Tonight is a study night."

We would not for one minute minimize the constant efforts by the public to impress upon our people the need for more highly educated persons. That is the process of impressing the general aims and needs of our culture upon our adults. But the process of carrying this out in the actions of the teen-agers is a separate if parallel aspect of this high goal.

Glick and Miller in their study of the relation between increase of incomes and education (in *American Sociological Review,* June, 1956) show that, based upon 1949 figures, men 45 to 54 years of age who finished high school made $466 more per year for each year of schooling than those who started high school and who dropped out before the senior year. That is a *fact* in the minds of the social scientists.

Our study is, however, one of how families in exceedingly complex urban surroundings translate this fact into a *motive* for a teen-ager to get him to complete high school. We are not arguing that all pupils have the requisite intelligence to finish high school. But we have sound reasons to believe that the half who do not finish high school include many who, if properly motivated, have that intelligence. Further, of the more than half of those who do finish high school and who fail to go on to college, probably motivation is again more important than ability.

chapter VII   IN THE PRECEDING CHAPTERS THE RELATIONSHIPS
between types of friendship groups and divorced or
arrest-history families have been examined in detail. Our conclusion was that the partial breaking of a family had a very close
relationship to a lack of a certain type of friendship intimacy.
"Good families," as measured by having a senior in high school,
decidedly avoided divorced, deserted or arrest-history families.
"Good" friend-families, measured by their common traits with
parent families, showed a similar tendency.

This must really be interpreted as a separation between
classes of good families, since we did not study "ordinary" or
"poor" families. Our study is of two types of good ones: Those
with all good histories, and those with blemishes from which
they had recuperated. Our comparison is between two categories,
one "good-good" and one "poor-good."

MORE THAN "BIRDS OF A FEATHER FLOCKING TOGETHER"

The analysis raises still another fundamental question. It is
whether we are studying merely association—"birds of a feather
flock together" — or a conscious effort on the part of good
families to avoid "bad" families. This is a question of great
importance. Were these families which we have called good,
always good, and have they always associated with their kind?
Or were they once mere ordinary people who accepted an ideal
or a vision of becoming better, and made an adaption which they
thought would help them and their children to become better?

If it is true that only a certain number of good families exist,
and that these only associate with other good families, then there
are very sharp limits to the creativity of any culture group.[1]

The theory of biological limits in the creativity of urban
populations was very popular at the end of the nineteenth and

---

[1] Good families reproduce less rapidly than poor families. The new
generation is not selectively bred from the good of the past generation.

the beginning of the twentieth centuries. Many scholars held the idea that there was a very limited number of possible creative persons. The idea was most comprehensively put by a scientist named Georg Hanssen in *The Three Population Stages* (Die Drei Bevolkerungsstufen).

According to Hanssen, the hard struggle for existence in country districts had eliminated many poor people and poor families. They failed to survive. The remaining high proportion of good families formed a sort of thick layer of cream living above the "milk" of ordinary and poor families. When, in the nineteenth century, the cities began to develop, the good families representing the cream, came to the city first. On arrival, they entered the middle groups in the cities, as contrasted with slum groups or those of the better districts. However, the increased struggle for material success in the cities was very rigid and psychologically debilitating. The good country-migrant families moved upwards or downwards very rapidly. If they moved upwards, they had to do so at the expense of late marriages, small families and reduced birth-rates. When successful, but with only one or two children, they made life too easy for their young. Their young being reared improperly could not carry on. Thus, it was from "wheel-barrow to wheel-barrow" in three generations for them.

According to Hanssen these "wheel-barrow" people were constantly and rapidly replaced by more and more good families from the country. These also followed the pathway to extinction of their predecessors. In time, all the cream was skimmed out of the country districts by urban migration of the good, and only poor people were left on farms. The cream was wasted in the cities and there was no further source for it left. This led to the decline of urbanized cultures because of lack of a source of leadership. Thus, according to this scholar, vast urbanization of a population was merely a prelude to its eventual decay.[2]

---

[2] This theory is annotated in detail, and examined, in P. A. Sorokin and Carle C. Zimmerman, *Principles of Rural-Urban Sociology* (New York: Henry Holt and Co., 1929) Chapters 23-25. Much of Spengler's *Decline of the West* was influenced by this idea.

FAMILY FRIENDS A NON-BIOLOGICAL METHOD OF
PROMOTING SOCIAL CREATIVITY

Our examination of the creativity of good families in America'
urban environment, which by now encompasses more than nine
tenths of the American people, leads to an opposite conclusion
Our results point to the fact that the new creativity of these goo
city families is largely a social matter. It is one of inspiration an
method, not of biology. These families have picked up a new se
of related values on "success," and on how to achieve it an
get ahead.

The high school families wish to protect themselves and thei
educational values. Consequently, over a series of years, they
seek to find and test friends who are like themselves. Graduall
they tend to eliminate opposite values and "trouble" from thei
households and, in doing this, to avoid mixing with persons o
conflicting values.

This is marked out by a number of facts. In every city a
families of the high-school parental groups associate with ver
few friend families who are marred by any bad trait (divorced
deserted, arrest record). In cities of the newer types, such a
those in the West, where scarred families are found more nu
merously in the parental groups, this avoidance is very severe

There are many more "signs" and evidences of this process o
seeking friends with like values and the use of this form of asso
ciation as a method of social creativity. We can test the assump
tion further by examining the process of "total avoidance" o
broken families—those broken for any reason, blameless or not
This can be done by an examination of the position of all familie
with remarried histories in the friendship groups. If remarriag
because of death of a spouse is treated the same, fundamentally
as remarriage for other reasons, (divorce, etc.) then we have
good case for our contention that families chose friends largel
only for creative purposes.

We are not contending that the high school families under
stand this process of like association and its beneficent influenc
on family life. People do not live rigid, logical, Socratically

directed lives. Instead they live by little prejudices, by little likes and dislikes. Their systems of total behavior, if integrated at all, are put together largely unconsciously. Our contention is that these petty likes and dislikes form patterns of "good" families. When viewed from the point of view of an outsider or from its total influence upon family life it may be called logical but to the families who do it, it is doing "what they like."

THE TOTAL AVOIDANCE OF BROKEN FAMILIES

Tables 35-39 give some basic data on this for all cities, and for all friends and student families for St. Louis, Mo., our typical city, where the 15,000 families were studied.

Table 35

FRIENDSHIP SIMILARITY AND
PROPORTION OF STUDENTS' PARENTS REMARRIED

*(Per cent of Families With At Least One Parent
Remarried Because of a Death or Divorce)**

Number of traits in common**	Boston	New Orleans	St. Louis	Denver	Omaha	Los Angeles
None	14.1	10.0	20.2	22.0	18.7	26.8
One only	10.6	8.1	17.6	19.9	16.7	24.6
Two only	7.4	11.0	14.8	15.5	15.1	23.3
Three only	7.5	8.5	12.6	15.3	15.3	22.2
All four	5.2	7.4	10.8	11.7	13.9	24.8
Total	8.2	9.1	14.5	16.9	15.7	24.1

* One or both parents in these families had lost a former spouse by death or divorce and they had remarried.

** The four traits are income, region of origin, religion and kin.

Table 35 gives the proportions of student families for every city in which either the mother or the father, or both, had remarried. They are classified in relation to the common traits they had with their friends. Each student was asked if his father or mother had married only once, or more than once. This gives us four classes of student families: (1) those in which it was a first marriage for both father or mother; (2) those in which it was a second or subsequent marriage for both father and mother; (3) those in which the father only had married at least once before; and (4) those in which the mother only had married at least once before.

These are families broken in any manner, either by death or divorce, or both, and hence does not differentiate between families broken by "acts of God" and "acts of man." The table shows that remarried persons, for any reason whatsoever, are most concentrated in those friend groups with nothing in common with each other. In the older cities, the friend groups in which the families had three or four traits in common showed less than half as many remarried persons in them. In the newer cities, the tendencies were the same but the degree of difference was not as great. This is for the parents of the students. It certainly shows the unwillingness of the non-broken families to associate with the broken. These conclusions apply to all families in all high schools studied.

Table 36

FRIENDSHIP SIMILARITY AND
REMARRIED PARENTAL FRIENDS BY CITY

(Percent of Friend-Families With At Least
One Parent Remarried Because of Death or Divorced Spouse)*

Number of traits in common**	Boston	New Orleans	St. Louis	Denver	Omaha	. Los Angeles
None	31.5	35.0	38.7	29.2	33.3	24.8
One only	13.4	17.8	23.0	20.7	18.3	23.1
Two only	8.3	11.9	16.7	16.7	13.0	22.3
Three only	8.6	11.6	14.0	16.9	12.0	19.5
All four	7.0	8.4	12.4	12.5	14.0	18.8
Total	10.4	12.7	18.0	18.7	15.7	22.3

* One or both parents in these families had lost a former spouse by death or divorce and had remarried.

** The four traits are income, region of origin, religion and kin.

Table 36 is also crucial. Here are the types of friends chosen by the students' parents. Here we see the striking pattern of avoidance of broken families. In Boston, 32 out of every hundred families with nothing in common with their friends were re-married whereas in the category of "four things in common" only 7 out of a hundred were remarried. This striking difference was true for every city with the differential being greater in the older cities than in the newer.

One of the reasons why the avoidance of broken spousal families was not as great in the West as in the East is the high prevalence of broken families there. We have repeatedly men-tioned the fact that our "good families" are distinctly much better and more highly selected than ordinary or poor families. Yet in the cities of St. Louis, Denver and Los Angeles, about one out of every five friend families had been broken by a former divorce, annulment or a death of a parent.

BEST-FRIEND-FAMILIES LEAST BROKEN

Table 37

FRIENDSHIP SIMILARITY AND PARENTAL FRIENDS
REMARRIED BY ORDER OF CLOSENESS TO PARENT

(Boston, Omaha and Los Angeles Compared for
First and Fifth Orders of Friends)

Percentages of Parental Friends of Broken Families (Remarried)

Number of traits in common*	——— Fifth friend ———			——— First friend ———		
	Boston	Omaha	Los Angeles	Boston	Omaha	Los Angeles
None	27.0	33.3	30.0	35.7	38.6	26.2
One only	12.3	15.7	21.4	16.7	22.3	28.0
Two only	8.6	13.3	21.4	10.1	11.5	22.8
Three only	8.2	11.7	18.4	8.1	13.6	16.8
All four	8.1	12.8	15.7	13.0	11.6	16.7
Total	9.6	14.5	21.0	13.0	14.3	22.8

* Traits are income, region, religion and kinship.

Table 38

FRIENDSHIP SIMILARITY AND STUDENTS' PARENTS REMARRIED BY ORDER OF CLOSENESS TO FRIENDS

(St. Louis, Mo.)

Percentages of Students' Parents Families Where at Least One Was Remarried Because of Death or Divorce

Number of traits in common*	First friend	Second friend	Third friend	Fourth friend	Fifth friend
None	24.8	21.6	24.1	17.3	19.9
One only	18.5	17.0	19.6	18.0	18.9
Two only	16.7	17.0	13.7	16.0	13.0
Three only	13.6	13.0	13.4	11.8	11.7
All four	10.4	12.1	10.7	9.2	12.7
Total	15.3	15.2	15.1	12.6	14.6

* Traits are income, region, religion and kinship.

Tables 37-39 concern the selectivity of parental friends among the remarried. A comparison of the selectivity of the first and most intimate friends with the fifth and least intimate friends shows that when the families picked their best friends they preferred those with unbroken spousal records. In other words, broken families tended to be concentrated in the least intimate groups.

The purpose here is merely to study forms of human intimacy among families and the influence of this upon the younger generation. Certainly no moral issue is involved when a man or woman loses a spouse by death. The problem is purely how families associate in order to achieve their aims in life.

Detailed data on broken families in each order of friendship for St. Louis, Mo. for both students' parents and their intimate friends (Table 39) show a clear picture of avoidance. (The pic-

Table 39

FRIENDSHIP SIMILARITY AND PARENTAL FRIENDS
REMARRIED BY ORDER OF CLOSENESS

(St. Louis, Mo.)

*Percentages of Families With at Least One
Spouse Remarried Because of Death or Divorce*

Number of traits in common*	First friend	Second friend	Third friend	Fourth friend	Fifth friend
None	33.4	33.8	38.6	42.2	51.8
One only	21.9	25.5	23.3	26.1	25.8
Two only	16.3	18.0	19.2	18.3	14.1
Three only	13.1	16.2	15.6	13.3	13.1
All four	13.9	10.0	12.2	15.5	11.1
Total	15.9	17.9	18.8	20.0	18.3

* Traits are income, region of origin, religion and kinship.

picture would have been very much more striking had we presented Boston rather than St. Louis.) Remarried friends were most prevalent in the casual (nothing in common) and in the far-away friends. First friends with four things in common—those most influential in the lives of children—were 13.9 per cent of the remarried friend families, while, among the fifth order of friends, with nothing in common, they were more than half the total (51.8 per cent).

We divided the broken spousal families (that is, one or both parents had been married more than once) into two categories—those in which one only had been remarried and those in which both had been remarried. The avoidance *pattern* was identical in each case. That is a characteristic of family behavior—mutual discoloration. The act of one influences all. The students' parents seemed simply to be avoiding bringing into their homes any semblance of broken social relations, no matter what the type of the broken relations might be. Insofar as possible the family and its intimate surroundings were being used to present a picture of "wholeness in life" to the children.

BLANKET REJECTION OF BROKEN FAMILIES

One of the most surprising things to us at first was this blanket avoidance of "broken families" without regard to "cause" and seemingly above and beyond any moral conviction. There were a certain small number of such units found in every friendship cell but these tended to be kept to a minimum. "Blanket rejection" is a term used here to mean the tendency to keep away all broken families without distinction (deaths, divorced, desertion, one remarried, both remarried).

At the beginning of the study we thought that persons with children might feel some doubts about associating with families where one or more parents were divorced. However, we thought that families remarried because of the death of one or more spouses would not come under this categorical ban and that they would circulate freely among the unbroken families.

Our surprise was to find that, where possible, unbroken families avoid all families that are broken. So far as we have been able to discover from this study, differentiation as to the type of breaking is not of great importance. Unbroken families try to avoid the introduction into their homes of divorced persons or representatives of families in which juvenile arrests are common. They also avoid those broken by death. Families as "whole institutions" generally make friendships most lastingly with families that are whole institutions.

This may probably be explained in part by the feeling of comfort and likeness which whole families have with each other and partly by their desire to present complete and untroubled pictures of whole life to their children. The more families have in common the less are families with broken records included. This is the trend in every city studied.

In Boston, for illustration, the student families with friends with whom they have nothing in common are broken in 14.1 per cent of the cases, but where all four traits are in common, in only 5.2 per cent. In St. Louis the figures are 20.2 per cent and 10.8 per cent. Every city has this same type of relationship.

Earlier we have said that association with similar persons has a "causal relation" with the characteristics of those families. That is, we have said that "friendship groupings by similarity of values" tended to reduce the divorce or desertion rates, to help avoid juvenile arrests, and to keep the teen-agers properly motivated so they continue in high school to the graduating class. We have made causal statements based upon the togetherness of facts. Now we explain part of the reasoning leading us to do this.

The reasoning is this. Similarity of friendship in any manner cannot influence the death rate. Hence we take these figures as to similar avoidance of *all* remarried families to mean "blanket avoidance." No matter what motives may underlie the matter, *"whole" families avoid "broken" families.* It is more than the "birds of a feather associate together" idea. It seems to be one of "keeping all troubled relations away from our door" so our children will not be disturbed in efforts toward higher goals.

We extend this proof when we study the percentages of broken families among the friends in each city according to the number of traits they have in common. Here avoidance becomes very noteworthy. The 14.1 per cent of students' families in Boston which associate with families with whom they have nothing in common find 31.5 per cent of those families "broken." The 10.0 per cent of families in New Orleans who have friends with nothing in common have 35.0 per cent of such families. In St. Louis a fifth of the families have one or more friends with nothing in common, but two-fifths of these types of friends are of the "broken" type. By broken type, to repeat, we mean that at one time or another the husband or wife or both in these families had had at least one other previous marriage.

This total avoidance of broken families means two things. First, breaking, without regard to cause, is a large handicap in successful friendship groupings. Second, whole families and broken families are very highly polarized. Broken families are clustered largely in the less intimate, the far-away and the occasional friendships. Both come back to the same causal relation-association of whole families with only whole families which facilitates child motivation.

AVOIDANCE GREATEST IN NEWER CITIES

The avoidance of broken families is a more severe problem in the newer cities than it is in the older. For instance, Boston has 8.2 per cent of broken families among the high school population, whereas this percentage doubles in Denver and Omaha and triples in Los Angeles. However, among the friends these families select we find a greater tendency in the newer cities to avoid broken types than in the older ones. The contrast is best seen if we note that Boston's 8.2 per cent of broken student families have 10.4 per cent of broken family friends whereas the 24.1 per cent of broken student families in Los Angeles have only 22.3 per cent. Broken family percentages in the high school population triples between Boston and Los Angeles, whereas in the friend population these only double. This means that avoidance increases more rapidly where the problem is greatest.

The major difference between the proportions of once broken families in the old cities and the new, lies in the higher divorce rates in the new. Death rates are about the same for similar age groups in all cities. Los Angeles has the highest divorce rate of all cities studied.

ALL HIGH SCHOOL FAMILIES BETTER THAN AVERAGE

Broken families in the high school population and among their friends are not the same as broken families in the total population. Broken families are more numerous proportionately in the non-high school population of ordinary and poor families. Our studies show this for every city. Unbroken families in cities with a high proportion of broken families apparently tend to avoid the unfortunate more rigidly than they do in cities with a low proportion. Here is further evidence for the theory of social creativity by selective association of families.

The typical patterns of avoidance of broken families are given in Tables 38 and 39 for St. Louis, Mo. First friends and intimate friends are less "broken" than far-away and less intimate friends, except where kindred are included. It seems that kinship overrules, in part, other feelings. Here "duty" supersedes "inclination." (This pattern of avoidance seems greater where both parents are remarried than where only one is remarried.)

Table 38 shows broken families have more trouble making intimate friends. When families select friend-families, they have a strong preference for unbroken ones. Take, for instance, the fourth and fifth friends with nothing in common with the parent families in Table 39. The percentages are 42.8 and 51.8 per cent contrasted with 13.9 and 10.0 per cent for the first and second friends with all four traits in common.

SUCCESSFUL FAMILIES HAVE BETTER FRIENDSHIP GROUPINGS

The analysis of these family friend groups shows that success in creating them, and their intimate nature, was exceedingly significant to the well-being of the families as measured by resistance to divorce, to desertion, and to juvenile delinquency and ability to climb up the economic and educational ladders. It is an important key to motivation control of children.

Successful families have more intimate family friends and have more in common with their friends than do unsuccessful families. This clear relationship between the similarity of family friends groups and mutual protection shows that the "good" social structure depends upon the "good" family and these two unite to strengthen each other.

The process pictured here statistically is the same as the living process stemming from each marriage. What these families have done is what every well-intended family tries to do everywhere once it is formed by mating. This teen-age child sees life through the eyes of the people with whom he associates. "Bad companions" and "bad friends" are held almost universally to lead to trouble for the youth. The family seeks to implant its "official" values in the child. In doing this it surrounds itself with similar friends. They do this because they like similar persons, there is less room for argument and clash, and their values are more or less close or identical.

Thus the child sees persons like his parents in his home

over many years. Not only that but when he goes into the homes of his parental friends, he meets there other persons, their friends, although not close friends of his parents. However, since the social organization of his parental friends is like that of his parental groups, he still sees persons greatly like his parents.

THESE TWENTY-FIVE FRIENDSHIP LAYERS HELP MOLD CHARACTER

As elaborated in an earlier chapter, the ordinary child has about twenty-five layers of similar friends about him. These tend to fix him in time and place and help establish his value system.

No matter what we read about the city, its mobility, its isolation, its contact between stranger and stranger, this is not true of the increasingly large number of families who are now becoming "civilization adequate" in our large cities. Somehow or other our sociology has given us a false picture of the fundamental and lasting social processes found in these cities.

The study also suggests the following: First, *the basic "social" family principle is that of common values.* Its values are not only unique but "purposeful" in terms of group existence in a difficult world. This unique, purposeful, common value principle begins with mating and extends thru the life history of the family and outward in family friends. It has traditionally been observed that children and grandchildren tend to follow both "good" and "bad" values of their predecessors. Happily married persons tend to have happily married children. Divorced parents have more divorced children. Our study shows this same principle holds from first and most intimate friend to fifth and least intimate friend. It operates in social space as well as in time from one generation to another.

This is why and how a family culture can change from one period to another. When people are increasingly warned about the difficulties arising from divorce, they eventually find the mechanism to decrease the divorce rate. When they become increasingly disturbed by the juvenile delinquent problem, they find the mechanism to minimize the proportion of juvenile delinquents.

To illustrate. During the first half of our century divorce

and delinquency rates have increased in the United States. Now they have become "social problems" of great significance and intelligent leaders want to know what to do. They seek to stem the tide by family counselling and by movements to rehabilitate delinquents. All these are necessary. But at the same time it is necessary to arouse the minds of people themselves in order to get them to use the family-closed-group as a preventative measure against the increasing occurrence of these divorce-and-delinquent risks.

Let us put it this way: There are those leaders in the family field who shrug off the problem of divorce and delinquency with the plausible statement that "these are the price we pay for the type of civilization we have." In other words *nothing can be done* except to treat the individual disasters when they arrive. An alternative would be to say high divorce and delinquency rates are not necessary evils. This would stimulate families to use the natural processes of social groupings to minimize their occurrence.

This leads us back to the "family polarization" idea. People seem afraid of that word. "Don't put it in your book because Aunt Minnie won't understand it." "Please don't use it on the television program today." But polarization is a necessary word because our family system is polarizing. That is, we have one current in our family system which has no particular antagonism to family disruption and accepts it as a necessary evil. It includes a small but noisy part of our people. Family conditions among this group are now getting worse and worse. It is becoming pretty much isolated because other families are not intimate with them.

The current moving toward the other pole contains the majority of American families. They have great moral antagonism to divorce, particularly in their own family groups and friends, since they feel that it influences their children. These are the great groups of families trying to produce high school and college graduates and doing it most successfully.

This does not explain all divorce and delinquency because some of it occurs everywhere and seems unavoidable.

Our civilization has been challenged greatly by our rise to world power and by the space age. We badly need the good current in our family polarization and we do not need the bad current. We need increased stress upon moral directives to everyday persons; we need to encourage them to avoid divorce and juvenile delinquency. For such persons, good family friendship groups is the great psychiatric force for character formation.

"Polarization" explains why we have a greater incidence of bad and a greater incidence of good families in our culture at the same time.

CAUSAL SIGNIFICANCE OF SIMILAR FRIENDS

The development of the principle of similarity in social space and its consequences shows that we have measured a fundamental "cause" in family actions. While we can expect some common values within a household to arise unconsciously and without choice, and expect children and their families to reflect the values of the parental organizations from which they came, yet when an uprooted people (migrants to the U.S.A. and to our cities) very quickly reassembles a similar outward family structure in a new environment, and when this new structure forms a consistent protection against divorce or desertion as well as against juvenile misbehavior, we take this to mean some conscious perception of actual cause and remedy.

This statement means that the choice of similar family friends is partly a deliberate act with some perception of its value in achieving at least two basic family purposes—sustaining the organization and preventing discoloration or stain arising from delinquency.

Thus our study convicts much of our contemporary family theory of misunderstanding the group nature of the family. We do not deny that the family is partly an allowable form of sex mating. It is that, but something basically more. It is a part of a working social system, both in terms of structure and values. We deny that the family is only a "unity of personalities," a simple nominalistic group. It is a means of extending the social system in fundamental structure and values.

As such it is a "real" group of private and unique values, and thus differs fundamentally from the general category, "unity of personalities." It differs from the general and nominal "unity-of-personalities" category perhaps more largely than any other human aggregation .

FAMILY MOTIVATION BASIC TO EDUCATION

chapter VIII THE TENDENCY FOR EACH SUCCESSFUL FAMILY is to gather about itself a small group of five or six other families which are like itself, as measured by kinship, intermarriages, neighborhood propinquity, common friendships, income class, origin and religious faith. We arranged our families in each city by pockets on a two-dimensional scale. The first dimension measured nearness of the families; that is, student family and first friend, student family and second friend and so on up to student family and fifth friend.

The second dimension measured the similarities of these families according to whether they had no trait in common, or one, two, three or all four. Thus, when one studies one of these tables, he has a name of comparison from the groups consisting of student families and their closest friends with all traits in common to groups of student families and their fifth friends with no trait in common. Our two-way scales measure simultaneously the likenesses of the families and their degree of impact upon each other.

In addition, we were able to evaluate these groups of families according to their success, or its lack, as measured by divorces and desertions, as measured by remarriage, and juvenile arrest histories. This adds a third or qualitative dimension to the above two.

Each table is used twice—once to show the quality nature of the student families in each pocket and once to show the goodness of the friend families in the same pockets.

Consequently, our method is a definitive fool-proof means of measuring simultaneously three variables or dimensions, intimacy, similarity and the success of families in maintaining good husband and wife and parent and child relations.

THE FIRST RESULTS SUMMARIZED

Briefly, our results have been as follows: In every city, in every degree of intimacy and in every measure of friendship similarity, the co-working of intimacy and similarity has been associated strikingly with success. That is, the more friends are like each other, the more successful they have been in avoiding divorce, desertion, juvenile arrest records and other phases of the breaking of homes and domestic relations. The more intimate families showed those results more strikingly than the less intimate groups. That is, in general these relationships were greatest for the nearest, or number one groups of families, and least for the farthest away, or number five groups of families.

As each table was reversed it showed the degree of success or its lack for the friend-families as well. In the intimate similar groups of friends, the index of success for the friend-families was greatest, and in the less intimate and dissimilar groups of friends, the success of the friend-families was least. Difficulty was always most prevalent among the far-away friends and among those most unlike the student families.

We have explained this relationship of success in the groupings among the friend-families by the fact that these are also good families. Although they have many other friends other than the student families, these other friend-families have been picked or selected according to the same principles and characteristics approved by the student families in making their friendship selections.

Thus if a child for any reason whatsoever happens to be in the home of a friend-family of his parents, and there meets one of their friend-families (which is not intimate with his parents) he also meets someone very similar in background and ideals to his own parents.

THE MATRIX OF CHARACTER

We call this group of intimate friend-families about the social life of the child his *"protective blanket"* or *character matrix*. It

protects him from an intimate knowledge of strangers and o
persons who have strikingly different and challenging value
from those of his parents. This protective blanket about these
good families most often consists of about twenty-five othe
families (out to the fifth friend of a fifth friend).

Assuming that there are five persons per family, this gives u
about 125 persons forming this typical protective blanket o
matrix of character.

Consequently, the knowledgeable social life of a child in
good family, until he finishes high school, consists mainly o
four parts or types of experiences. First, are those from his con
tacts with his parents and siblings, whom he knows best. Second
are those with about 125 other persons remarkably like his par
ents in backgrounds and values. Third, he has around him th
"official behavior" of certain "public" persons such as schoc
teachers, religious leaders, pastors and priests, scout, club an
summer camp leaders and others. These are under very rigi
public supervision as to what they can and can't do to the chil
or how they must act before him and with him. Their impact o
him is very circumscribed as, for example, teaching archery
arithmetic, language, sports, Sunday School lessons or catechism

Fourth, and finally, he has a secondhand social environmen
from the radio, television, newspapers, books, movies and publi
spectacles. These are very much censored by "public" (i.e.
largely parental dominated) opinion as well as directly by hi
parents.[1]

It is in this sort of situation that character is formed, ideal
grow up and personalities are motivated. The variables insid
this social matrix are the *ideals of the parents* as to what the
wish for their children; the *capacities of the children,* biologica
or otherwise to live up to these ideals; and finally, cracks, o
seams, or *breaks in the social matrix* which permit conflictin

---

[1] The authors have discussed the so-called "peer group" in other studies
With "good" families, they believe the peer group is controlled by th
parents, and thus without the significance sometimes accorded to it.

values in to confuse the child and make him doubt the wisdom of the previous norms of conduct laid out before him.

EDUCATION OUR MAIN THEME

Now we have to go on to relate this social organization of good families to the educational process. The educational ideal and its implementation by the social process of the family is our main theme. We have, in this century, moved into a new era in which the "civilization-adequate" man is an educated person. Our question is how this new projected achievement is facilitated among the young.

Each era calls for a new "ideal type" of man. Roughly we may sketch out the eras of the modern world since the Western dark age (VI to X centuries) by the naming of some of the newer ideal types of persons added in each period. A few of these are feudal liege man, handicraftsman, merchant guildsman, businessman, manufacturer and capitalist. The new era into which we are now entering will probably emphasize more than anything else, the highly literate technician and scientifically-educated man.

However, it is to be understood that a change in the ideal type of man from era to era is one of emphasis and not of total substitution. Certain traits are essential to being just human and are human prerequisites in all eras. These include the human, social and moral virtues of an everyday type. Our theory concerns only added traits which fit a man for the technical, scientific and organizational problems of this new atomic-age civilization.

Furthermore, the emphasis upon the educated technical and organizational man for the new era does not imply in the least that this education is a substitute for the "human virtues" mentioned above. It was customary in the nineteenth century, when the people of the Western world were first trying to get out of their medieval illiteracy, for many enthusiasts to claim that the universal ability to read and write would solve *all* social problems. That was not so and is not so. An educated thief is more dangerous than an illiterate one. The thesis developed here does not attribute any moral virtues to education per se. Rather it is a simple idea that the new era requires a more highly educated universal person for the economic and social system into which we are entering.

It should be kept in mind that the need for education in the future is not a call for only technicians and engineers. Technically trained persons, illiterate from the human point of view, cannot understand and manage the society which we are now creating for our future. We need labor leaders, artists, religious leaders, educated females in many technical and non-technical lines, musicians and all other kinds of humanistic leaders on a large scale.

Neither does this mean that all persons can or should get college degrees. Those in the lower half of their class in intelligence tests probably could not benefit greatly from college educations and some of those who drop out in grammar school could benefit little from high school educations.

We are concerned mostly with the further educating of the members of that half of humanity which have high scores on intelligence tests and fail to finish high school or try for college.

INCREASING EDUCATION

The goal of literacy, or the mere ability to read and write was reached in American culture sometime in the early twentieth century. Our regular census, beginning in 1940, no longer reported statistics on literacy. The general assumption was that nearly everyone could then read and write. Compulsory school attendance laws applied in every state of the nation. In 1947 it was estimated that there were less than three million illiterates among persons over fourteen years of age. These were primarily southern rural farm Negroes or foreign-born who came here from very illiterate regions.

But literacy alone is not sufficient in this new world into which we are entering. Increasingly we need men and women on a larger scale who have high school, college, and professional training. These standards are essential for the world of instantaneous communication, science with its probings into the atom and outer space, as well as for the higher level of social requisites.

We may illustrate this increasing need for higher education by some facts about the growth of the proportions of the population in various types of schools. In 1890, before the onset of this new era, only seven out of every one hundred persons fourteen through seventeen years of age was in a high school as contrasted with 77 in 1952. This is an increase of eleven times in 62 years. As late as the class graduating from high school in 1940 (entering in 1936-37) only 579 of every thousand who entered high school graduated, but by 1952 this had increased to 616 out of every thousand. In 1870 less than two out of every hundred persons attended a college or an educational institution higher than the secondary schools. At the turn of the twentieth century, this rate was still only four per hundred. In 1951-52 it was 23 persons out of every hundred or a sixfold increase.

In 1932, of every 1000 children in the fifth grade we eventually received 786 in the freshman class of high school, 455 high school graduates and 160 in the freshman year of college. But the group which was in the fifth grade in 1944-45, put 848 of each thousand in a high school freshman class, produced 522 high school graduates and 234 college freshmen by 1951-52. Thus the group entering in the fifth grade in 1944-45 furnished an average of 62 per thousand more high school freshmen, 67 per thousand more high school graduates and 74 per thousand more college freshmen than those persons entering schools twelve years earlier. The point is not only that education is increasing, but that higher education is increasing more rapidly than that further down.[1]

THE WHY OF EDUCATION

There are several explanations of this increasing higher education which is in progress not only within the United States but in other western countries and now in Soviet Russia as well.

---

[1] All these data are from the *Statistical Summary of Education, 1951-52,* U.S. Office of Education, Washington, D. C.

The older explanation was that it was to a considerable degree a "cultural" attainment which, due to modern productivity, we could now afford for more and more of our children. A second partial claim was that since modern society no longer used child labor as in the early rural days and in the old-time factory system, children were held in the schools increasingly in order to keep them out of trouble. Concerning these two contentions we have little to say except to point out that the rapid rise of a great and expensive cultural institution such as our higher education—secondary, college and professional school—must have back of it fundamental and not surface causes.

Including private and parochial secondary schools, the United States had 26,929 secondary schools in 1951-52, and these with their 8,372,107 pupils required the services of 373,807 class room teachers. During that year there were 198,447 full-time equivalent faculty members in our institutions of higher education. Such a large and costly institution as this, most of which has proliferated during the last twenty-five years, cannot be considered to exist without excellent reasons.

One of the first signs of the fundamental nature of the demand for increasing education in a culture such as ours is the increased economic rewards being paid to those who graduate from high schools and colleges. Some computations of this have been made by Paul C. Glick and Herman P. Miller of the U. S. Bureau of the Census. These statistics are necessarily very crude, and are based upon material for 1949, so that they are already outdated. They assume that men twenty-two years of age in 1949 would live only as long, on the average, as the survival rates for that year. We know that our average life expectancy is increasing. They also assume that these men, in the future would make the same incomes that men of similar education in the advanced age groups were making in 1949. We know this is an underestimate because national and per capita income and productivity have been increasing rapidly and show signs of continuing to do so.

However, their estimates, even though low for the two reasons above, gave the elementary school graduate a life-time expected income of $116,000, the high school graduate $165,000, and the college graduate $268,000. This computation, rough though it is, makes high school graduation as of that year worth 50 per cent more than only grammar school education, and college graduation worth 231 per cent more than grade education. (These statistics were based upon what people of different ages and educations were making in 1949 as they reported them for the 1950 census.)

THE DECLINE OF THE UNSKILLED LABOR CLASS

Back of this economics, however, is something more fundamental yet, a cultural need. Our civilization has moved from back-power to brain-power; from direct production to indirect by use of machinery; from natural raw materials to synthetic; and from unskilled labor to skilled technicians and engineers.

The white people who settled America were mostly farmers and peasants from Europe. They came here with simple tools, and cleared the forest and tilled the fields. Their occupations were traditionally those said to be done by persons with "strong backs and weak minds." Then after the Napoleonic wars a new stream of migrants started coming again from Europe. Forty million more Europeans came in the century from 1840 to 1940. These millions also were nearly all manual or unskilled laborers seeking the jobs which the older settlers no longer wanted, such as digging the Erie Canal or building railroads and factories.

Now, however, we have educated ourselves out of the category of unskilled labor and embraced entirely new techniques. Unskilled labor as a component of our population has been dropping in significance for almost a century, moving slowly downwards until World War I and dropping very rapidly since. Our manpower experts classify our employed population as of 1950, very roughly as follows. Unskilled workers, 12 per cent; semi-skilled workers, 20 per cent; managerial workers, 11 per cent. This last category of managerial workers includes teachers, technicians, professional engineers and scientists, but these highly literate persons together make up only one per cent of the total working population.

STRONG MINDS REPLACE STRONG BACKS

The strong backs have been replaced, in a large degree, by machinery. Agriculture is the latest example of this replacement. In the early days of the nineteenth century, nine persons out of ten were on farms. Now there are about forty-five million households in the United States and of these, only two million are on farms of economic significance. On these two million farms, trucks, tractors, power plants and the numerous less-than-five horsepower specialty machines are doing most of the former manual work. Jobs formerly done by hand, not capable of being performed by machinery, are now increasingly being accomplished by chemistry. Different chemical sprays are now even doing much of the job of weeding truck gardens and cotton fields, the last real strongholds of hand labor.

In order to achieve this newer "roundabout" method of producing our living, men had to encourage their children to seek educations, and train themselves for different types of skilled and technical jobs in factories, service plants, mines, laboratories and the other institutions which furnish the tools and substitute products needed. The more technical industrial processes become, the more education and the more trained and educated workers were required.

Along with division of labor, or the roundabout method of producing old things, synthetic industry has arisen. Wood pulp, from which spring the rayons, and coal, the source of nylons and other synthetic fabrics, have made great headway against cotton, wool and linen. The plastics made from petroleum compete with the former wooden products. Petroleum is now cracked and reassembled into our gasolines and fuels. In a large degree the artificial rubbers from oil and alcohol compete with the product of the plantations. The taking of natural products apart and reassembling them into new and useful other things is now an industry valued at billions of dollars annually.

All of these processes are impossible except in a civilization of highly literate people in which more and more of the naturally qualified persons must mount higher and higher in the educational ladder. They do so to understand the new technical processes of fabrication, and, beyond that, join, where possible, in new research and development. Thus the educated person and the educational process is *the* something which is the key to the era of the future.

THE TECHNICAL MANPOWER SHORTAGE

Since World War II we have had considerable discussion of the manpower shortage. This term seems an anachronism to a society with more than four millions of new births each year (4,318,000 in 1957), or with its vast record of unemployment in the early thirties. The term really means a shortage of educated and trained persons—technical personnel.

Many persons believe we are in a race with Soviet Russia to turn out scientific and trained personnel. The recent launching of rocket satellites by Russia brought this sharply home to us. Those concerned about Russia think we are wasting much of our intellectual potential because not more than half the young persons with good native intelligence finish college. They feel that the high schools of the country are failing to offer sufficient basic training in mathematics and the fundamentals of science. They contend that scientifically trained personnel should not be taken into the armed services but should be utilized in the basic creative production processes. They have increased prestige and pay for scientists and engineers.[2]

---

[2] See *Scientific Monthly,* March, 1956, for a very worthwhile symposium on this subject by four of the nation's leading scientific educators, Eli Ginzberg, Edward A. Fitzpatrick, Howard A. Meyerhoff and Eugene M. Kulischer.

While this particular group of scholars are not pessimistic, they did note that the number of engineers in the Soviet Union were 540,000 as contrasted with 560,000 in the United States, 337,000 physicians and medical technicians there as contrasted with 400,000 in the United States,

Apart from our rivalry with Russia, the shortage is great if we look at our own peaceful needs, and think in terms of the next one or two decades, with our growing population, rising standard of living, vast consumption of natural resources and the growth in complexity of our industrial processes.

In teaching, in scientific research, in agricultural and industrial problems, in medicine, nursing, forestry and mining, to mention only a few, grave shortages of personnel are already predicted by 1960 or 1965. One can see them prospectively in the present scramble for college graduates. In earlier generations, the college graduate had to look for a job. The time spent in seeking employment was a sort of post-graduate course forced on him with his degree. Now employers come increasingly to the colleges to interview the graduating class. Formerly if a young man was soon to be liable for military service, no employers were particularly interested in him until after his tour of duty. Now firms are offering to start a man with as little time as a month before service in the hope that he will like his employer and return after military absence. In the words of a personnel executive of one of our large corporations, "things are not like they used to be for technically trained and educated young persons."

This argument need not be carried further. The educational process has come to the forefront in our modern culture. It has done so because our culture now demands highly trained persons in all walks of life, technical, political, legal, moral and social. This is not a substitute for the early emphasis upon honesty,

---

and 857,000 with college degrees in education as contrasted with 1,300,000 in the United States. The relative problem in Russia is claimed not to be a shortage of professionals and unskilled labor, but rather the lack of artisans and skilled labor.

Following the example of the Russians' use of the trained technicians of the satellite countries, these scholars suggest we integrate our talented persons with those of the other free nations, and thereby gain from borrowing and cross fertilization. As freely as we now import raw materials, they suggest we import leadership and brain power. Going to extremes, neither of pessimism nor optimism, these scholars convincingly underline the necessity for a large movement to find and train more brain power.

reliability and sincerity but an addition to those traits of the good citizen. The present pressure for an increase in educated personnel will become steadily greater in the coming decades.

THE NEW ERA MAN NEEDS EDUCATION

Thus we have moved into a new civilization in which the culturally adequate or socially valuable person is the highly literate individual, and this is reflected by the increasing proportions of persons in the high schools and colleges. It is clear this process of moving up into life via the educational ladder is now the basic creative social process. If we find out the mechanisms by which this process is encouraged and made to grow, we are brought immediately into the constructive and living aspect of our culture.

A measure of the demand by a technical culture such as ours for more and more educated persons is the advertisements for engineers and technically trained men, the statistics on the needs for more physicians, the radio and television campaigns for recruitment for the nursing profession, and the attitudes expressed by educators on all sides that "a high school education is not enough."

As an illustration, let us examine the advertisements for engineers in the *New York Times* for Tuesday, March 20, 1956, during the annual meeting of the Institute of Radio Engineers. The *Times* for that day had forty-five display advertisements, ranging from boxes covering seven square inches of space to full half-pages. The total advertisements covered about two thousand square inches of display advertising. They offered jobs in practically every state in the country. These advertisements featured high pay; security; advancement; adventure and excitement ("the daring approach . . . probing into the dark recesses of the unknown"); "paths to success," companionship and respect ("he needs men to work with to respect his abilities—and whose abilities he, in turn can respect"); "top professional assignments"; "forging ahead"; "relocation expenses paid"; "tuition reimbursement plan for advanced study"; "cooperative plan for a greater retirement income with company paying over 50 per cent"; and dozens of other inducements. While this particular edition came at somewhat of a special time in New York any large daily paper any day now has numerous similar display advertisements for technically trained men.

To understand the advertisements, let us look at the cohort of American children, two and a quarter million strong, who entered the first grade in 1940-41. If all had stayed in school through college and graduated, we would have had an equal number of A.B. degrees in the spring of 1956. Factually we didn't. Probably less than one in six or about 18 per cent graduated from college. However, let us look at the process all the way from first grade to college.

About 75 per cent or three out of four reached the eighth grade and graduated. By the time of the senior class in high school only about 50 per cent were still in school. If we leave out of consideration the one student in four who dropped out in the course of grade school, we have one more to account for in the first three years of high school. (Grade school years are those of compulsory education nearly everywhere in the United States. A large proportion of those leaving grade school may be spoken of as *selective,* if we define the term broadly to include defects of character, family background and intelligence as the selective factors. The selection includes most of those who are handicapped in mounting the educational ladder.)

HIGH SCHOOLS AND FAMILY MOTIVATION

In our opinion, withdrawals during high school are mainly a failure of *family motivation.* It is more motivation than cost. The cost to the families in keeping children in school is the value of the alternative earnings of the children if they go to work and give the money to their parents. Since, however, work permits are not generally granted until 16 years of age, except in hardship cases, the family loses possible income only from the 16- and 17-year-old groups. Fundamentally, the main factor here keeping children in school is family motivation.

With college educations, cost is a much more decisive factor. No matter what the motivation is, someone has to raise from four to twelve thousands of dollars in college expenses, in addition to and above the economic loss to the individual and to his family if he is not gainfully employed in these four years. It is true he will, on the average, make the money back and more too, if he graduates from college, but that is a promise which can seldom be banked against immediate needs during these four years, if funds from parents, scholarships or other sources are lacking.

Obviously the crucial age of family inspired or controlled motivation, in which the selective process has already operated, and the economic cost has not become insurmountable, is in the high school years, roughly the age groups from fourteen through seventeen. In this period adolescence is ordinarily passed, compulsory schooling laws let up, the child assumes the size and wilfulness of a young adult. In this period the aims of college or further education seem far away compared with immediate jobs and pay in the world at large. This is the period where time preference by youth (taking a long time viewpoint) is needed most and in which, with their immaturity, they have it least.

Even though a high school education alone is not sufficient for many current needs, one out of four who start high school drop out *in the high school itself* before reaching the senior class. Our analysis leads us to think that this failure to climb has something to do with family motivation and organization. To study this we secured the data from the high school seniors already summarized, in part, in the preceding chapters.

Success and failure will henceforth be measured by one thing alone, the ability to keep the child in high school to the senior class. In the previous chapters we used other indices. In the succeeding chapters we will analyze the results from the educational viewpoint and tell how we think successful families succeeded in keeping their children in schools until the senior high school classes, and, by inference, a good many of the reasons why others failed.

HOW FRIENDSHIP GROUPS CONTROL
EDUCATIONAL MOTIVATION

chapter IX   THE MAJOR OVERRIDING HYPOTHESIS OF THIS STUDY
is that intimate groups of similar family friends are
the instruments used by parents in the motivational control of
the teen-ager. The consolidated picture of life or illusions they
give the child lead it to try to achieve group standards. Since
going ahead in high school is a major gain in life, according to
these standards, the families are thus successful in seeing him
continue to the senior year. The parents and friends may not
understand this influence clearly, but they use it.

THE TEEN-AGE DECISION

Our previous analysis has suggested that most of the children
mentally unable to complete high school educations have been
eliminated from the schools before reaching sixteen years of age. At
sixteen, or thereabouts, comes the turning point in the child's life.
Will it be upwards or out? The main deciding factor is the feeling
of the child as to which course he wishes to follow.

Back of that feeling is the child's interpretation of what his
parents wish for him and of the standards of his "group." Up
to this time of his life his "group" has consisted mostly of the
persons around his home. If the adults are like his parents and
share the values of his mother and father, he feels that a clear-
cut and unchallenged attitude in favor of continuing school backs
him up. He is not "in a lonely crowd" if we may use the words
of a recent popular work elaborately misinterpreting our recent
American culture. He is protected from confusing pressures from
a confused community. If the adults around his home are like his
parents, then most of his child friends are similar to him and
share in his developing attitudes toward life.

We are assuming here that the parents are aware of a need for continued schooling for their children. Even if they have not read any census reports on higher earnings and social rewards for the graduates and the more educated persons, they have themselves seen this in their own occupational lives. An ideal or ambition must exist in the parental minds.

PARENTAL IDEALS PRIMARY

However, given these ideals among their parents, the question is how these turn into actual motives in, and achievements by, the young. It should be clear at the beginning that by the time the child is sixteen, the major goal of motivation is already gained, or the damage is done. Matters of motivation are not instantaneous. The earlier years of the child's life are the formative ones and these are already passed when the final decision is made.

However, it is one thing to state our hypothesis: the continuation of the student in the school process is due to an early form of friendship organization of the families, long continued, in which the ideal of movement up the educational ladder has implanted itself. It is quite another thing to prove it.

We have no *direct* knowledge of the ideals of the parents of the families we studied, or of their friends, except as an assumption. We merely assume that they wished their children to go upward on the educational ladder or these would not have continued in high school. We also have to assume that the friend-families shared this ideal of continuing education or they would not be allowed as intimates around the household or would not have had so many other measured things in common with the student families.

PROOF OF FRIENDSHIP SIGNIFICANCE

Consequently, our logical proof of the relationship between the constant surrounding of the children by these matrices of similar friends (same objective traits and same ideals), and the continuation in high school has to be made upon indirect grounds and by use of complex analysis.

We are in the same situation as were the medical men when, earlier, they sought the "cause" of malaria. They knew that malaria was very prevalent in wet (swampy) and hot regions and not prevalent in dry and cold regions. Their first hypothesis was that the swamps with their "bad air" brought about malaria. They did not know then that the mosquito was the carrier and that the swampy and warm dampness was responsible only in the sense that it enabled more mosquitoes of the malaria-carrying type to breed.

We know that the parental families are organized most typically into strong small groups with intimate similar friends. Now how can we probe into this situation or prove what we suspect, namely, that the friends are the educational "mosquitoes," and the intimate friendship groupings are the "warm swamps" in which the educational mosquitoes thrive.

FAMILIES IDEALS ARE "BUNDLES" OF INTEGRATED AIMS

The first probing into this question leads us to point out that family values, as any system of values about a social organization, are not unitary but "bundled" together in an integrated or *syndromic* sense. (A syndrome is a group of things which appear and grow together because they are related to each other and interdependent. The symptoms of a cold thus form a syndrome. If one has a real "Grade A" cold, he has nearly all the symptoms in the syndrome such as fever, headache, sore throat, loss of appetite and excessive mucous discharge.)

Our contention is that the main difference between family types as "poor," "ordinary," and "good or successful" lies in the degree to which the better types possess all the syndromes of "familism" and are able to carry these out. In this present syndrome of good familism we put the promotion of motivation of the child toward completing his high school education as a major factor.

A good family starts with a so-called "proper" relation between man and woman. Even if it starts otherwise, it often belatedly gets to be a proper relationship.[1] Instead of remaining ordinary acquaintances or casual friends, the man and woman become deeply interested in each other and decide to enter into a life-long relationship, cemented by a public ceremony in which they agree to love, honor and obey "till death do us part." They become husband and wife.

Out of this proper relation they become parents of children and embark upon a long-time process of rearing, protecting, supporting and preparing these children for life. The whole process is a "syndrome of familism." The numerous qualities in this syndrome of familism come from our mores about proper family behavior and by a very comprehensive code of family law. At no time in history has the law and custom specified as clearly and voluminously the obligations of the parent-child relation as it does now in modern society and in our country in particular.[2]

FAMILY IDEALS ARE FUNCTIONALLY INSEPARABLE

All social organizations consist of bundles of syndromes of aims and values. Being a good citizen, a good soldier, a good workman or a good club member consists in the faithful ad-

---

[1] A very good study of "inadvertent familism" turning out relatively well afterwards is Eliot Slater and Moya Woodside, *Patterns of Marriage,* Cassel and Company, London, 1951.

[2] The proofs of this statement are documented in detail in Carle C. Zimmerman and L. F. Cervantes, *Marriage and Family,* Chicago: Henry Regnery Company, 1956, pp. 65-131; L. F. Cervantes, *And God Made Man and Woman,* Chicago: Henry Regnery Company, 1959, pp. 184-270. Roscoe Pound has pointed out that, in the long history of family law, societies have ordinarily left family internal affairs very much unspecified, believing that religion, good mores and common sense would take care of such things. However, the collection of unsigned essays prepared by various governmental departments for use at the 1948 *White House Conference on Children* pointed out that the volume of law as to parental obligations to children had grown tremendously in the United States during recent years. On this matter see The Association of American Law Schools *Selected Essays on Family Law* (Brooklyn: The Foundation Press, Inc., 1950), Chapter I by Pound *et passim.*

herence to and fulfillment of not one but a group of interrelated principles or values. This is an ordinary (but important) sociological principle.

Within the family as a social organization (and it has always been the most important and most highly integrated unit in society) we may discern two classes of values: (1) those holding the unit together, and (2) those showing how it should function. In the husband-wife relationship, for example, the two classes concern those holding husband and wife together and those prescribing the duties or functions of the proper husband and proper wife.

Similar syndromes of values exist about holding parent and child together and as to the duties or functions of the proper parent and proper child. *Sui juris and alieni juris,* "age and nonage"; "consentable and non-consentable persons."

Now we cannot consider the holding of husband and wife, of parent and child, together as one form of behavior and the positive functioning of these persons as husband, wife, parent or child as another. Husband and wife are held together because they can function together and not separately and similarly with parent and child. In the case of parent and child, the parent protects, guides and fosters the preparation of the child for life, and the child's function is to yield to this protection, to grow up under it and to become a good citizen.

HUSBAND-WIFE SUCCESS "COLORS" PARENT-CHILD SUCCESS

The mere remaining together and the coexistence of husband and wife as spouses is only one side of the coin. The functioning value of husband and wife is the other side. "Holding together" and "functioning" in their disparate but united roles cannot be separated either for husband and wife or for parent and child.

However, this is not all. Parent-child forms of behavior are important functions of husband-wife behavior, and the two are interrelated. Parent-child behavior, or those syndromes connected with the assumption of the roles of parent and child, follows husband-wife behavior in time; ordinarily men and women become husband and wife before they become parents.

In a similar way husband-wife behavior is a function of parent-child behavior. When a society wants to adjust or change parent-child behavior it first readjusts husband-wife behavior. To give a simple and concrete case, when the Russians had trouble with juvenile delinquency—the gangs of orphan "wolves,"—in the second and third decades of this century, their first, biggest step was to legislate strongly against divorce in the new law codes of 1944.[3]

Thus, anything which has a material influence upon husband-wife relations will also influence the parent-child relation. This proposition may also be inverted. However, since husband-wife relations precede parent-child ones, disruption of parent-child may not have as drastic an influence upon husband-wife as the reverse. Putting it simply, a divorce is more likely to cause a parent-child estrangement than a juvenile arrest is likely to bring about a husband-wife estrangement.

A divorce, desertion or delinquency is known in family sociology as *discoloration*. Once a family is established, an extremely good act by any member has a good influence upon all members and a harmful or disgraceful act by any member "discolors" all members. This "discoloration" is the old time incitement and *raison d'etre* of the family feud. "By harming (shaming?) a member of my family, you have stained (discolored) me and I must take vengeance against you and your family members." One bad act tends to discolor all.

FAMILY FRIENDS AND SCHOOLING

There is a close relation between positive and negative actions in husband and wife, and parent and child, relations. Having a child continue in high school is a positive function of child protection and of family success. Failing to continue in school is

---

[3] On this read R. Schlesinger *Changing Attitudes in Soviet Russia— The Family,* London: Routledge and K. Paul, 1949; Cervantes, *And God Made Man and Woman,* pp. 192-200.

negative. But the positive and the negative are again two sides of a single coin. "To abolish the negative, we must accentuate the positive."

We have now reached a stage in this analysis where it is possible for us to see that any conspicuous factor which helps or impedes the husband-wife relation, helps or impedes the parent-child relation. Furthermore, anything which influences either of these or both helps or impedes the child in achieving such aims as continuing in school.

In other words, if association with intimate similar friends keeps down the divorce rate, it will also reduce the juvenile arrest rate. And if it does these two things conspicuously, it will facilitate the acceptance of the parents' ideals by the children. If these ideals are more schooling, the important influence on continuing in high school to graduation will be the nature and types of family friends seen intimately within the home.

If all this seems complicated it can be put in one or two sentences. Namely, parents with an ideal for their children, such as school continuance, can most *thoroughly implement that ideal in the minds of the children by surrounding this household from the beginning with similar friends who also possess this same ideal*. Secondly, juvenile continuance in school is the positive side and juvenile arrest the extremely negative of the same form of behavior.

To prove the above contentions that the types of intimate family friends are responsible for continuing high school, we now have to show that the absence of this friendly matrix is highly correlated with juvenile arrests and other family failures. Then by studying all these cases carefully we can tell with considerable accuracy how and why the intimate family friends contribute to the successful motivation of the child. First we prove our case and then we seek to find *why* it is true.

AN ANALYSIS OF RESULTS

This leads us to a reappraisal of our results reported so far. We started with successful families as measured by their ability to retain at least one child in high school to the senior or graduating class. We asked teen-age seniors to characterize their own families and give similar objective information about the friend-families of their parents as these had been seen in their homes. We studied about ten thousand parental families and about fifty thousand of their friend-families.

The first results showed that each family tended to have about five intimate friend-families. Most of these friend-families had been visiting in the parental homes between ten and fifteen years so that the children had known these friends continuously since before they themselves had started the primary grades of school. Of all the people these students had known (their *total life impressions* from persons other than their parents) they knew these friend-families the best, the longest, and had seen them most frequently. *Thus, the great totality of all the impressions of life other than parental had been received by these children from these friend families.*

A second phase of the study showed the high proportions of kindred in these friend-families. Under our law and social organization, kindred *families* have no legal right in the houses of relatives, and enter only by voluntaristic consent. Consequently, we have reason to believe these kindred were there, and had been there, only because they were liked and invited there. In other words, they were an asset to the families of the seniors and *vice versa.*

A third aspect was the way of meeting friends other than kindred. The meetings of these families had not been in business offices, in churches, in schools or in other circles where the principles of selection of associates were dominated by non-family agencies. Rather the meetings with these friends came about largely through other friends or the neighborhood contacts. All our evidence points to the fact that the friend-families other than kindred had been selected by the original families likewise by a careful process in which fairly factual information would be available so that a reliable choice could be made.

We rated the parental and friend-families according to four

indices of similarity; namely, kinship by blood or intermarriage, religious confession, region of origin and economic status. We reasoned that people who were kindred, or of the same religious confession, or of the same region of origin, or of the same income grouping would tend to "think more alike" and to feel more alike than persons not in the same category. In other words, we reasoned that similar friends would have more attitudes and values in common.

FAMILIES WITH BEST ORGANIZATION MOST SUCCESSFUL

Our next step was to arrange the parental and the friend-families into five categories, those with nothing in common, only one trait, only two, only three and all four. For each step of increasing similarity we computed the divorce rate and the juvenile arrest rate for each group of the families, both the original and the friends.

As indicated earlier in this chapter we have reason to believe that divorce is the opposite of good husband-wife relations, and juvenile arrest the direct opposite of good parent-child relations. Anything which impedes the opposite or bad relation tends to leave a vacuum to be filled by the good relation. The way to prevent bad behavior is to keep children busy at good behavior. If juvenile arrest is impeded by good friends, then school retention is promoted.

Good husbands and wives make good parents. Good parents try to do the best they know and can for their children during the formative years. If good friends are related closely to both reduced divorce rates and to reduced juvenile arrest rates, then there is considerable reason to conclude that the friends help make the matrices in which the children are motivated.

We found for *every city* and for *every order of friends in every city* that the increasing intimacy of similar friends was associated strikingly and outstandingly with the reduction of both divorce and juvenile arrest rates. This was true not only for the parental families but also for the friend-families. There were no exceptions to any phase of this. There were no exceptions for friend groups, for order of intimacy, for order of similarity or from city to city, including Stillwater, Oklahoma and Morgantown, West Virginia, not presented in detail here.

If good families and good children were a disease, we would have to conclude that all who associated in these friend groups, whether parental family or friends, or the children in the families, had caught the "disease" from this constant companionship. Since it is not a germ disease but an achievement, we attribute the achievement to the working out of ideals in this kind of similar intimate association in the home surroundings.

Thus, from the evidence so far, we are forced to attribute the creativity of these people fundamentally to the ability of these human matrices to foster and to encourage the implantation of the good ideals of the parents concerning husband-wife, parent-child and child-schooling achievement.

THE LACK OF STRONG SOCIAL ORGANIZATION

The previous section analyzed the cases in which the strong social organization of similar intimate friends apparently prevented the intrusion of challenging values into the matrices about the homes. Thus, we claimed that these groups "protected the family." We may speak of them as being similar to strong hulls of good ships which keep out the water of the seas and thus help them make peaceful voyages toward a destination.

Now we can show this by taking the opposite cases. Such an example of opposites is the family in the newer cities where the tumults of social relations tosses these matrix ships about more violently than in older settled regions. Another is the new and unsettled people in any city, as measured by the fact that the fathers of the families were long-distance migrants—not born in the regions of the cities themselves, but in other regions. Third, is the case of the remarried parents, remarried for any cause whatsoever, whether because of court separation or of death of one or the other. Finally, we have the well-to-do and the poor. In these four cases we may speak of a loosened social organization.

FAILURES IN THE NEWER CITIES

In the newer cities of the West where all rates for difficulty among families are greater than in the older cities of the East, we may expect, if our theory is correct, greater struggles against broken families and greater avoidance of them where possible. This is exactly what has been shown by our study. When our cities are arranged according to the "relative newness" of the settlement there of the masses of their present populations, we find this greater avoidance of broken families increasing as we pass from "old" to "new."

For our hypothesis to have passed such a test is of capital import. City comparisons are treacherous because many conflicting circumstances can arise in such a large social aggregate. For instance, the Mormon community around Long Beach and Los Angeles is a very homogenous and old settled one. The Negroes in St. Louis have increased greatly there since the big manufacturing boom of World War I. Many of Boston's latest groups of migrants have come from various countries in recent years.

Nevertheless, the facts are clear. Any social situation of extreme heterogeneity and difference of views seems to force a closing of ranks about the families. Thus, since the Boston population studied contains about six in one hundred families with deserted or divorced histories (a low rate), association by chance would give them friends with that rate of divorces or desertions. That is exactly what we have, 6 per cent among student families and 6.2 per cent among friends. However, St. Louis, Denver, Omaha and Los Angeles have much higher rates for divorce in the general student population but very reduced rates *relatively* among the friend-families.

This reversal of trend is particularly outstanding for cases of juvenile arrest. Boston has juvenile arrest histories among 6 per cent of the student families and 5 per cent among the friend-families. Los Angeles has rates of 15 per cent among the student families and only 8 per cent among the friend-families.

FAILURES AMONG LONG DISTANCE MIGRANTS

A second type of proof concerns those families which came from outside the region in which the city is located. Take St. Louis as an illustration. It is a regional city of the Midwest. Of its total families studied 63.4 per cent came from the Midwest but those with juvenile arrest histories were only 36.5 per cent from the Midwest. Other regions showed the opposite based on region of birth of fathers.

Table 40

ST. LOUIS: ARREST RECORDS AMONG FAMILIES WHICH HAVE UNDERTAKEN LONG DISTANCE MOVES

Percentage of all families from		Percentage of all juvenile arrests
Pacific	4.1	10.5
Rocky Mountains	2.9	7.0
Southwest	7.7	7.0
South	12.5	23.0
Northeast	4.7	6.0
Outside U.S.A.	4.7	9.5

In this city, there was only one minor exception, the Southwest. All other regions showed the same results. Apparently, the very fact of origin outside of the region had been an influence preventing the making of strong similar friends to protect the families against juvenile arrest histories.

FAILURES AMONG THE POOR AND THE WEALTHY

The third sort of proof given earlier in this work concerns the relative frequency of juvenile arrests among the poor and the very well-to-do rather than among those middle groups above $2,000 in income and under $10,000. Poor people live where it is difficult to keep children out of the hands of the police because of slums and crowded neighborhoods. Consequently, their arrest rates are high because it is very hard there to protect youth. The well-to-do, on the other hand, apparently are able to give their children sufficient funds for them to get away from home surroundings and into trouble more often than do other families. As a result, even with the greater amounts of "fixing" and "smoothing over of trouble" and protection which these people are able to give their children, still they have higher arrest rates. This we have already reported. These figures are based upon the total families studied, or sixty thousand.

FAILURES AMONG THE BROKEN FAMILIES

Finally, we have the case of the remarried families, including those brought about by deaths of spouses. This rift in the network of social relations is related closely to juvenile arrest histories. In a later study we will have to examine the details of this more closely in order to understand the exact process.

Nevertheless, we can now say with absolute certainty that it changes the nature of the friendship groups away from the normal pattern pictured for the good families and in this way makes arrest histories possible.

Here our case is clear. These once broken families are good ones. Our proof is that they have been able to survive two sorts of danger or disaster, broken spousal relations and high arrest histories. In spite of this double trouble they have survived and kept their children in schools. Thus, the trouble with children in their cases is in the social organization because they have shown that they have good motives.

INTERFAITH MARRIAGE AND FAMILY CONFLICT

chapter X WE HAVE NOW PROVED THAT FRIEND GROUPS PRO-
tected the families. Groups with similar backgrounds
seemingly were enabled to do this by force of the psychological
barriers they erect against the entrance of conflicting values into
the mental arena of the family members particularly of the children. Thus families with similar friends tended to be more successful in rearing their children according to the patterns the parents
wished. This was simply because the "social group" which the
child encountered in his formative years was composed of members who were remarkably similar in values. The "world" he
came to know intimately and to respect was of one pattern.

It has also been pointed out that our evidence was, to a
considerable extent, seemingly of an "indirect" type. That is, we
proved that the absence of similar friends was associated strongly
with husband-and-wife disruptions by divorce and parent-child
disruptions marked by arrest records. The presence of friends like
the parents was associated with very low divorce and arrest rates.

Further the point was made that being "good" as a husband,
a wife, a parent or a child was not compatible with being "bad"
as such. The two are contradictory. They are incompatible traits
in the same behavioral patterns. On the one extreme is the family
with the deserted or divorced history. On the other is the very
good family which has a husband and a wife trying to make a
success of the total domestic institution. At one extreme is the
family with the arrest history. At the other is the family whose
children go through high school without any such records. The
friend grouping that minimizes divorce and arrest records also
provides the proper motivation of the child.

Since the presence of similar friends about the family is highly
associated, in every case studied, with very low rates for divorce
or juvenile arrests, it is evident that the friendship patterns prevent conflicts with the "good ideals" these parents have adopted.

MIXED-RELIGION MARRIAGES

In order further to prove this analysis, we now make a completely different approach. We disregard entirely the family friend patterns and consider only cross-marriages in which the husband and wife are of separate religious faiths. If the absence of similar good friends about the family makes it easier for challenging values to get through and confuse the child, so also do many of the cross-faith marriages. The cross-faith marriage tends to make it easier to bring alternate value systems into the domestic circle. Such a crevice in the family value walls starts at the beginning of the marriage and before the child is born (if the husband and wife do not reach a sure compromise). This early crack in the psychological armor about the child tends to widen when his faith-choice comes up and to allow other conflicting values to come into the situation.

Table 41

RELIGIOUS CONFESSION OF FATHERS OF ALL FAMILIES STUDIED

(Percentages by City)

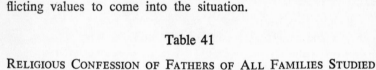

City	Protestants	Catholics	Jews	Other	None	Total Percent	Total Number
Boston	15.7	73.1	6.4	3.0	1.8	100	6,824
New Orleans	18.7	63.9	2.5	7.3	7.6	100	8,352
St. Louis	29.0	46.5	5.0	10.3	9.2	100	13,284
Denver	43.6	38.3	3.4	7.5	7.2	100	6,737
Omaha	36.5	44.8	4.6	8.2	5.9	100	7,061
All ∫Percent	28.4	52.7	4.4	7.7	6.8	100	
₊No.	11,984	22,249	1,867	3,272	2,886		42,258

In order to study this we took all our families, whether student or friend, for which we had the religion of the husband and of the wife, and arranged them in groups according to faith of the husband. This gave us two categories for each faith, Protestant husbands who married Protestant wives, Protestant husbands who married women of different beliefs, and so on through Catholic men, Jewish men, "other religions" men and "no reigions" men with the same or different confession wives. Each group of the 42,258 marriages for which we had information was put in two categories by city, those who married wives like themselves in religion and those who did not. From these data we can test the groups according to whether they married "in" or "out" of their religions.

The basic data for the families is given in Tables 41-48. Since we did not tabulate the information for wife's religion for Los Angeles, we analyze only Boston, New Orleans, St. Louis, Denver and Omaha, which reduces our total number of families to 42,258. The subtraction of the Los Angeles group also gives our total somewhat of a greater preponderance of Catholics, since Los Angeles was the most Protestant of our cities. Our group in this analysis numbers 11,984 Protestant men's families, 22,249 Catholic, 1,867 Jewish, 3,272 "others" and 2,886 claiming no religion. Protestant men make 28.4 percent of the sample, Catholics 52.7, Jews 4.4, "others" 7.7 and "nones" 6.8.

THE IMPORTANCE OF THE COMPARISON
BY MIXED RELIGIOUS MARRIAGE

Now we are ready to clinch our case by studying these families, not according to friendship groupings, but according to another principle which, nevertheless, contains our previous test. This is a comparison of families according to whether husbands and wives married someone of their own religious confession or made a cross-marriage. Since religious groups all have very strong family doctrines, whether Protestant, Catholic, Jewish, Christian Scientist, Mormon or Pentecostalites, the making of a cross-marriage could not in itself be responsible for an anti-family action such as a divorce, a desertion or an arrest history. All the religions studied consider divorces, desertions and juvenile arrests as "bad."

Consequently, if a religious person marries someone of another religious group, both groups being strongly opposed to family failures, the higher record of the failure among the cross-marriages cannot be due to a "bad" family doctrine. Rather it must be due to the mixture of faith, making an easier "aperture" for conflicting values. Such cross-marriages seem to make the psychological background of the family members, particularly children, more open to conflict and negation of values.

RELIGIOUS PERSONS HAVE STRONGER FAMILY IDEALS

As we show, religious people are more pro-family or "familistic" than non-religious persons. Those families in which both husband and wife have no faith or religious confession show rates for divorce and arrest histories from two to ten times higher than the Protestant or Catholic rates for these in the same cities (Tables 43 and 46). However, when a man of the non-faith group marries a religious ("pro-family") woman, their cross-marriage is significantly more conducive to family success as indicated by rates of divorce, desertion and arrest histories. The reason for this improvement is due in part to the religious wife's bringing religious devotion to familism. If this were not so, we should expect this cross-marriage of a no-faith husband and religious wife to have the same increased divorce and arrest-history rates as other cross-marriages.

We emphasize this to bolster our previous statement that the cross-marriages of religious persons, although showing a higher percentage of family failures, do not do so because of the absence of sound family doctrine. The fathers and mothers in these families are both hoping for the development and preservation of the domestic unit and for the proper rearing of children. However, since many of them carry religious controversies within the family circle, even involving the grandparents of the children (who by definition have differing religious confessions), the child begins to doubt somewhat all values of his parents.

A FINAL TEST OF OUR THEORY

Thus in differing religious confessions at the time of marriage, we have the materials to put our basic theory to a final test. Our theory was that a conflict of values in the immediate psychological realm of the child, particularly among those closest to him, meant a wavering in his determination to accept unchallengingly the ideals of his parents. In cases where spouses have differences of views, and do not resolve them in clear-cut, unhesitating fashion beforehand, the clash makes an aperture for doubt in the mind of the child. This aperture opened by clash in faith widens apparently to include the totality of family ideals resulting in increased estrangement rates for husband and wife and parent and child.

CROSS-MARRIAGES ARE VERY COMMON

In Table 42 we give the percentages of mixed marriages among the 42,258 in our sample. The total is 15 per cent. This

Table 42

PERCENTAGES OF MARRIAGES OF MIXED RELIGIONS

(Grouped According to Confessions of Fathers)

City	Protestants	Catholics	Jews	Others	None	All
Boston	29	5	14	26	61	11
New Orleans	30	8	53	36	64	20
St. Louis	12	8	21	20	60	16
Denver	11	11	27	20	52	15
Omaha	10	9	23	22	44	13
Total	15	8	24	24	57	15

percentage shows that the mixing of faiths within the homes of successful families is much less than the general public's, but, nevertheless, is very common. Since most of these families had sufficiently resolved their conflicts to carry on as successful domestic institutions, we are led to believe that the failures are where the two sides of the family (husband's and wife's) were unwilling to compromise on religious problems in the interest of family unity.

The questionnaires indicate that the groups with the least cross-marriages are the men, both Catholic and Protestant. One element in this pattern is that men of whatever religion more readily than women abandon their faith in cross-faith marriages. In the total sample, 8 per cent of the Catholic men had non-

Catholic wives varying from 5 per cent in Boston to 11 per cent in Denver. However, since Boston (68 per cent Catholic) is the most Catholic of the cities studied, the low rate there seems due primarily to the more frequent opportunities for Catholics to meet Catholics, whereas in Denver (24 per cent Catholic) somewhat the opposite is the case.

The Protestant men with non-Protestant wives totaled 15 per cent of the sample varying from 29 per cent in Boston and 10 per cent in Omaha. Here again, in the total numbers of contacts between males and females, it is more likely that a Protestant youth would associate with a Protestant girl in the newer cities of the West where Catholics are not as numerous.

Boston requires a further special word. The organization of Catholics and Protestants there is different from that in the other cities studied. In Boston the historic leaders of the Catholic Church are of Irish extraction. Succeeding waves of Catholics, particularly the Italians, had not much in common with the Irish except Catholicism. Before the Catholic Church became aware of this situation and began to develop "ethnic parishes," many Italians had fallen away from the Catholics to the Protestants. Consequently there are probably many more "recent" Protestants in Boston than in the other cities. For this group of Protestants to marry back into the Catholic faith is not as great a step as it is for the people of more ancient Protestant faith in other sections of the United States.[1]

---

[1] On the problem of the Italians and their disaffection with Catholicism in the United States, see A. Palmieri, *Il Grave Probleme Religioso Italiano Negli Stati Uniti,* Firenze, 1921. The outstanding student of mixed religious marriages in the United States is Reverend John L. Thomas, S.J., of the Institute of Social Order at St. Louis University. Thomas has summarized his studies in his book *The American Catholic Family,* Prentice Hall, Inc., Englewood Cliffs, New Jersey, 1956. The most recent signal contribution to the subject is James H. S. Bossard and Eleanor Stoker Boll *One Marriage Two Faiths: Guidance on Interfaith Marriage,* Ronald Press Company, New York, 1957. In this Bossard records his notes on the problem, its increase, and means used for resolving its conflicts based upon his experience studying it since 1925. An analysis of the total influence of cultural and religious mixing upon other groups and upon the

Table 43

MARRIAGES IN SAME FAITH AND DIVORCE OR DESERTION RATES

Percentages in Marriages Where Both Were

City	Protestant	Catholic	Jewish	Other	None
Boston	7.3	4.3	4.7	4.9	45.9
New Orleans	11.4	5.1	33.4*	13.9	48.6
St. Louis	9.8	4.2	8.6	12.2	20.0
Denver	5.5	6.1	8.4	7.7	18.0
Omaha	6.4	3.8	12.6	9.9	24.2

* Based upon 108 cases.

RELIGIOUS MINORITIES MOST PRONE TO CROSS-MARRIAGES

Jews, who are a small minority in all our cities, show the greatest tendency for cross-marriage of any of the three orthodox religions. The total rate for Jewish men marrying Gentile women is 24 per cent. Here again, where kin Jews are most numerous, as in the Boston sample with 6 per cent, they show the least tendency for out-marriages, only 14 per cent. In other cities where Jews are less numerous the percentages are greater. The Jews in our study made up 2 per cent of the school population of Denver but they and their friends reported 27 per cent of Jewish males married to non-Jewish females.

We cannot pay much heed to New Orleans in this part of our analysis because we do not know the principles of selection which led to the make-up of the parochial school population, which was the only one studied there.

The "other religions" have a high proportion of out-marriages, 24 per cent. This is consistent with their minority position, within the population in every city. However, we cannot analyze them in detail because, as has been suggested throughout this work,

---

Italians in the United States is given by Carle C. Zimmerman, "Some Aspects of Collective Settlement of Italians in America," a chapter in a book published in 1959 by the University of Rome as a memorial to Corrado Gini.

the category "other religions" embraces unlike groups, probably mostly Mormons in the West, Pentecostalites in the center, and Christian Scientists in the East.

In some tentative tabulations we disregarded the classification as "other religions" and threw the whole group into the Protestant confessions. This re-analysis, however, did not change a single conclusion made from leaving them separate so we discontinued this approach.

The "nones" are most prone to intermarry with religious persons. The total average for our study is 57 per cent. This is partly due to the fact that "nones" are a miniscule section of the population: also professing no standard type of confession is most frequently a philosophical position of the male, rather than of the female, and such males are often forced by lack of other opportunities to marry religious females.

We emphasize this high prevalence of cross-marriages among the people studied for several reasons. Apparently it is something which will increase as other differences between the segments of the American population are lessened or become minimized. As we show later it tends to bring conflict more easily within the family. However since it will not lessen as a factor in American marriage, our problem is to help make the persons who do engage in inter-faith marriages understand their vulnerability insofar as successful family life is concerned.

CROSS-MARRIAGES INCREASE DIVORCE

Tables 43 and 44 summarize the rates as among cross-

Table 44

INTERFAITH MARRIAGES AND DIVORCE OR DESERTION RATES
Based Upon Husband's Religion (Wife Different)

City	Protestant	Catholic	Jewish	Other	None
Boston	11.0	13.5	25.4	26.0	25.3
New Orleans	14.6	13.0	57.4	21.6	23.6
St. Louis	18.9	12.0	44.4	27.0	16.5
Denver	17.7	15.9	48.3	18.9	21.1
Omaha	16.9	16.7	62.2	16.7	10.6

marriages of divorce or desertion. The first gives the rates for each confession where both husbands and wives were of the same faith. All the groups marrying in their own faith show very low rates, except those in which a man claiming no-religious faith is married to a no-religion woman. Normally the spousal troubles in families of orthodox faiths, even including the Christian Scientists, Pentecostalites and Mormons, is limited to less than one in ten or one in twenty of the marriages.

Some exceptions to low rates exist in New Orleans due presumably to the selective nature of the parochial high schools. Protestants who send children to these parochial schools in New Orleans have a rate of 11.4 per cent of spousal troubles (among themselves and their friends). This may be due to the use of the parochial school training to compensate for conditions in families where troubles have already appeared. An added motive is that, in New Orleans, Catholics are reputed socially higher than in most other American cities, going back, as a group, to the eighteenth century.

The high rate for the Jewish group in New Orleans, as reported in our sample, is among friends of the student families, since no student reported his family as Jewish. These 108 families are a minority of Jews in a city where there are very few anyway. Presumably they were already largely alienated from orthodox Jewish circles, since they were intimate friends of Gentiles. In Omaha, where Jews in our school sample were only 3 per cent, the divorces of Jews married to Jews were also slightly higher, representing about 13 per cent.

In New Orleans and St. Louis the divorce rates for the "other" religious groups were slightly higher than normal. Our own particular opinion as to the reason for this is that these are representative of certain poverty-stricken economic strata of the population, since we think they are mostly Pentecostalites. We have noted all through this study that the "poor" have more family trouble than the middle classes, partly due no doubt to the slum areas of the cities in which their lack of means forces them to live.

Our purpose is to compare Tables 43 and 44. The first significant fact about them is the rise in divorce percentages among the families which are classified as cross-married. Let us remember the families are classified by the religion of the husbands and the percentages are of divorced or deserted histories for those families in which the husband is of the designated confession and the wife of another.

When the marriage is a cross one based upon religious confession the divorce rates of the Protestant groups rises two or three times the height of the pure religious marriages. Among Catholics it rises three or four times when the marriages are crossed. Among Jews, who are more clannish than Catholics, the rates rise normally five or six times when the marriages are crossed. Among the "others" the rates rise two to three times when a cross is made.[2]

WHEN NO-RELIGION MEN MARRY RELIGIOUS WOMEN DIVORCE DECREASES

This comparison has particular value. We may show it by anticipating the dramatic "Divorce Or Desertion" division of Table 47.

In every city except Denver, the drop in divorce percentages when the non-religious husband is married to a religious wife was sharp and drastic. In Denver the rates for divorces was 3 per cent higher when "nones" married religious. This might seem to be an exception to our general finding: when non-religious men marry religious women the marital disruption rates are lessened. But Denver has an unusual situation. Denver's Spanish-American citizens are a depressed minority with all its disadvantages and social psychopathies, but one whose women are not prevented from marrying into the non-Spanish-American

---

[2] In the work by Bossard and Boll, *One Marriage: Two Faiths,* pp. 70-73, an analysis of Judaism and inter-faith marriage is given. Orthodox Jews customarily excommunicate the cross-married person in a ceremony called *Cherim* unless the Gentile becomes a convert. Since these cross-marriages reported here are not of converts the shunning may be responsible for the lower economic standing of cross-married Jews reported in Table 48 discussed later.

majority. The Spanish-American group is the low ethnic one on the social totem pole, presenting the typical marginal-man social profile: constituting less than 10 per cent of the population, the group (Spanish-American names) account for 60 per cent of the registry of the State Industrial School for (Delinquent) Boys, receives 50 per cent of the children's aid funds, constitutes 30 per cent of all admissions to the General Hospitals. At least one out of four Spanish-American children lives with neither or but one of his parents. Ninety per cent of the youths with Spanish names who have entered high school within a twenty-year period, according to a survey of the Denver Mayor's Commission on Human Relations, did *not* graduate. Contrary to the experience of the Negro minority, however, the Spanish-American minority finds little difficulty in intermarriage with the "Anglos," which brings us to the apparent exception of our statistics. Spanish-Americans are overwhelmingly Catholic. The contention that Catholicism to the majority of this ethnic group is a cultural rather than a theological commitment cannot be entertained here. But we do know that when a female member of the Spanish-American group marries a male who has no religious commitment, disintegrative mores of her group do not allay the conventional disintegrative marital picture of those who profess no religion. Her minority and marginal mores are not completely compensated for by her religious faith.

But the slight exception in the case of the Denver Spanish-American minority in no way invalidates the original and general principle derived from our study: when a non-religious man marries a religious woman, the religious background of the woman is the decisive influence in the lower divorce and desertion rate.

CROSS-RELIGIOUS MARRIAGE INCREASES ARREST RECORDS

Table 45 gives the arrest-record percentages for the families which consisted of husbands and wives of the same faith. Table 46 gives the same for cross-marriages. The religious marriages ordinarily shows very low rates for arrests, whereas the "nones"

Table 45

MARRIAGES IN SAME FAITH AND ARREST-HISTORY RATES

Percentages In Marriages Where Both Were

City	Protestant	Catholic	Jewish	Other	None
Boston	5.4	4.2	2.5	4.2	47.9*
New Orleans	18.0	4.2	33.0	20.6	47.0
St. Louis	5.8	4.0	5.1	7.0	20.7
Denver	4.6	7.7	11.1	6.2	13.1
Omaha	5.7	6.8	11.0	8.3	22.5

* Based upon 48 cases.

married to "nones" ordinarily had very high rates. In Boston the Jews married to Jews had the lowest rate, 2.5 per cent. The Catholics and the "other religion" groups (probably mostly Christian Scientists) were next with 4.2 per cent. Protestants, who are a minority in Boston, had a rate of 5.4 per cent if they married Protestants. The "nones" (based upon forty-eight cases) had a rate of 47.9 per cent when they married "nones," or almost every other family.

In the West where indifference to religion is more common the arrest rates among the "nones" married to "nones" is less than half the Boston rate but it still is strikingly high, about 21 per cent in Omaha and St. Louis and 13 per cent in Denver.

In the West, particularly Denver and Omaha, the Jewish rate is highest, the Protestant lowest, with Catholics and "other religions" in between. Part of this higher rate of the Catholics in these two cities is connected with the minority position the Catholics hold in the populations there. Another part is due to the recent immigration of Catholics of the Spanish-American group. Many came from Mexico as laborers, either legally or as "wetbacks" *(braceros)* and decided to stay. These new migrant people are still extremely low socially and economically.

The cross-marriages, with the single exception of "none" males married to "confessing women," show higher arrest rates in every city and in every religious group except the Protestant

Table 46

INTERFAITH MARRIAGES AND ARREST-HISTORY RATES

Based Upon Husband's Religion (Wife Different)

City	Protestant	Catholic	Jewish	Other	None
Boston	6.6	8.5	26.7	14.0	17.6
New Orleans	12.3	12.8	62.2	21.4	23.3
St. Louis	11.1	9.8	41.1	16.1	10.4
Denver	8.7	10.9	40.0	17.8	12.0
Omaha	10.7	13.0	58.2	17.7	16.7

cross-marriages in New Orleans around the parochial school group.

Here as noted before, the cross-marriage to Catholics by Protestant women is in many cases an "upward" marriage socially. Protestant cross-marriages in Boston, as suggested earlier, are most often a "return" to a faith traditional in the families and hence have little disturbing effect upon the arrest situation. In St. Louis, Denver and Omaha the cross-marriages of Protestant males with non-Protestant females show a double arrest-record rate in the families.

Catholic men married with non-Catholic wives show doubled or tripled arrest-record rates for their children in every city. Jews, however, married to Gentile women have the most disturbed situation. In Boston, St. Louis, Denver and Omaha, the arrest-record rates in families with a Jewish father and a Gentile mother are from four to ten times higher than in the non-cross Jewish marriages.

WHEN "NONES" MARRY RELIGIOUS WOMEN ARRESTS DECREASE

Here again we have to note the distinction between the "nones" married to "nones," and "nones" married to religious women. In three cities, Boston, New Orleans and St. Louis, the influence of a religious mother is associated with a reduction in the arrest-record rates by more than a half. Boston comes down from 47.9 per cent to 17.6 when the marriage is a cross of a

"none" with a "confessing" wife and mother. St. Louis comes
down from 20.7 per cent to 10.4. New Orleans families of this
type show drastic reductions in arrests. The reduction is less,
but still significant, in Denver and Omaha.

Table 47

DIVORCE-DESERTION AND ARREST-HISTORY RATES

(When Non-believers Marry Religious Women)

Percentages by City

| | Divorce or desertion | | Juvenile arrest histories | |
| | *None to none* | *None to religious wife* | *None to none* | *None to religious wife* |
City				
Boston	45.9	25.3	47.9	17.6
New Orleans	48.6	23.6	47.0	23.3
St. Louis	20.0	16.5	20.7	10.4
Denver	18.0	21.1	13.1	12.0
Omaha	24.2	10.6	22.5	16.7

Table 47 is a special tabulation comparing the arrest-history
rates and desertion-divorce rates for each city for the "none-to-
none" and the "none to religious wife." We present this comparison in a consolidated table because it is striking and unusual.

MARRIAGE AND ECONOMIC STANDING

We secured the income groupings of the families but if we
presented all the details for each city it would be very complicated. In Table 48, however, we do give the proportions of
pure and cross-married families who are in the income groups
above $5,000.

Our purposes in presenting this table are several. We wished
to know if in general it was a poorer or wealthier group which
was cross-marrying. Further we sought some idea of the differences in wealth of the religious groups. Thirdly, what happens
economically to the Jews, "others" and "nones" when they cross-

marry? Considerable information exists as to the influence of family troubles upon reduced income-making capacities. Does religion have anything to do with the economic capacity of an income producer?

Our conclusions are as follows. The wealthiest group generally are the Jews and the poorest are the "other religions" and the "nones." The "others" in Boston are up to the average in wealth but these, as explained elsewhere, are different from the "others" in other communities. However, the picture is very complicated; Jews who marry Gentiles are either poorer at the start, or being shunned in business connections, do not do so well. As explained earlier, Jews are very rigid in their marriage customs.

Table 48

PERCENTAGES OF FAMILIES WITH INCOMES ABOVE $5,000 PER YEAR

(By Religious Confession of Husbands and Type of Marriage)

City	Protestant		Catholic		Jews		None		Other	
	Pure	Cross	Pure	Cross	Pure	Cross	Pure	Cross	Pure	Cross
Boston	53.7	52.3	53.7	51.0	71.1	56.7	52.3	44.2	43.7	55.3
New Orleans	48.7	50.8	49.5	47.9	64.3	42.3	41.7	49.8	46.1	50.6
St. Louis	48.0	55.7	58.4	50.6	78.7	51.8	38.1	48.9	48.9	49.3
Denver	55.4	43.1	44.0	48.4	69.7	62.2	40.8	43.2	38.7	46.0
Omaha	55.2	49.3	52.5	47.4	75.1	53.5	41.4	46.0	41.6	54.0

One thing is as expected. A "no religion" man with a religious wife is better off on the average than if he does not marry such a woman. Thus we find that religious wives are valuable not only from the standpoint of less divorce and lower arrest-rate histories in the family, but also from the economic point of view.

CONCLUSIONS

In this chapter we have tested our earlier conclusion that the wall of common values about the family and its children was a great protective device. We believed that this was true because similar friends kept the family members out of trouble by serving as means of psychological containment.

Now we have tested this idea further by taking religious cross-marriages as measures of the easier possibility of breaching the walls of values. That is, when the family becomes a religious battleground, other conflicts can easily enter into the family. Our results are the same as the earlier ones.

Persons who cross-marry in religious faith can bring conflicts of values within the home. If these are not resolved the result is higher divorce, desertion and arrest rates. The exceptions occur when a non-believer marries a religious woman. In these cases the marriage, as measured by divorce, desertion, arrest rates and financial success, is helped.

Finally orthodox religious people are more successful in family life than the non-orthodox and the skeptics.[3]

---

[3] Cross-religious marriages have been the object of a number of extensive statistical studies. Among these might be mentioned those by M. L. Barron, J. T. Landis, J. L. Thomas, Ruby Jo Kennedy, James H. S. Bossard, Harold C. Letts, Harvey Locke, Georges Sabagh and Mary Margaret Thomas. Cross-religious marriage varies by faith (Protestants and Catholics high and Jews low) and by ethnic groups. A marked ethnic group, such as the Spanish-Americans, tends to cross-marry less than unmarked ethnic groups. Where people are a minority in a region, they tend to cross-marry more. Every study reports more conflict in religious cross-marriages than from marriages within a faith. This is reflected in higher rates for divorce, desertion and juvenile troubles. Our study, which bears out these conclusions, is merely to supplement the general theory that problems of families increase where it is made easier to have differing value standards which become subjects of conflict within the homes.

THE SOCIOLOGY OF FRIENDSHIP

chapter XI   SINCE THE BEGINNING OF HUMAN THOUGHT, THE nature and significance of friendship has been stressed in social thinking and in literature. Some of the greatest and some of the most, and least, socially inclined, have discussed friendship. Francis Bacon (1561-1626), who never was a friend and consequently had few if any friends, wrote beautifully about it. Our earlier Greek philosophical writers, our Old Testament historical books, and our modern sociologists have written at length about the nature of friendship, and its influence on human conduct.

THEORY ON FRIENDSHIP

Among the early Greeks, Homer used friendship and its disruption as the key to the changing course of the Trojan war. The disruption of the friendship between Agamemnon and Achilles over a camp follower caused Achilles to withdraw to his tent in anger, and led to the near destruction of the Greek forces. The slaying of Patroclus, Achilles' life-long friend, by Hector, stirred Achilles to fight again, with the eventual downfall of Troy.

Writing about the Greece of some three centuries later, the poet Hesiod, in his *Works and Days,* made friendship the key in his analysis of good social relations:

"When on your home falls unforeseen distress
Half clothed come neighbors, kinsmen stay to dress"

Aristotle (c. 330 B.C.) devoted the two most important and influential books (VIII and IX) of his famous *Nichomachean Ethics* to an analysis of friendship. He summarizes the whole of Greek thought upon the subject, and repeatedly refers to Homer to emphasize that friendship between well-intentioned people was essential to a well-working society.

ARISTOTLE'S ANALYSIS OF FRIENDSHIP

Aristotle said that friendship had been considered by the Greeks as one of the basic factors in the creation and working of a society. He held that it was a virtue or "connected with virtue." Friendship was necessary for life, since without it, all the other things of life were useless. The rich and powerful needed it because their wealth and prestige could not be kept without friends. When afflicted with poverty and "all other adversities, men (then) think friends to be their only refuge."

This philosopher widened the conception of friendship to include in it the basic essence of the bond of all "social communities." Hence his analysis took in all forms of social relations including those between the governing and the governed and between business men or traders, as well as simple "mutual affection, mutually known" between persons on the same level who had no obvious economic interest in friendship except for the "kindliness between persons who reciprocate it."

This latter kind between good persons was to Aristotle "the perfect friendship." Those friendly relationships for gain, as between traders, and for governing, as between the social classes were imperfect types. Other friendships for "pleasure or for profit" he considered also imperfect, even though they approached the perfect type. The perfect friendship was between equals. It "results from a similarity of some sort" and takes time to grow, or until the friends "have eaten the requisite quantity of salt together."

One other point of great importance in the analysis by Aristotle is his giving the greater social significance to friendship among older persons than among the younger. He held that friendships of the younger were more often a "matter of impulse and based upon pleasure"; consequently the young "conceive friendships easily and quickly dropped them." Friendships are "very liable to dissolution if the parties do not continue alike and it is in the nature of the rapid change among the young that the persons, once friends, do not continue alike.

We particularly mention this point from his analysis because our study is on the influence of like parental friendships upon their children.

THE BIBLE ON FRIENDSHIP IN SOCIAL RELATIONS

After these observations upon the social significance of friendship in the Greek folklore and philosophy which dominated Western thinking from its earliest period to about the sixth century of the Christian era, our next great reservoir of social-relations-thinking is the Christian Bible. This has been the standard of conduct for most Westerners since the Vulgate edition codified by Jerome in the fifth century of the Christian period. The Bible gives no special section completely devoted to an analytical summary of friendship, as did Aristotle's works, but it reaches about the same conclusions. The numerous references to friends therein warn about the bad ones and praise the good ones. This is a differentiation similar to Aristotle's between "perfect" and "imperfect."

The Golden Rule "do unto others as you would have others do unto you" is a guide toward universal friendship. The "Good Samaritan" was a person who did a friendly act to a needy stranger. The whole idea of the world-embracing role of the new religious message was one of seeking friendship among all persons. Christianity arose in the decaying polyglot Roman Empire and no other rule of conduct could do as much towards making diverse men humane to one another. Christianity stressed two bases for friendship, both familial in concept. Men were to love one another because they were "children of the same heavenly father who makes the sun to rise on the just and the unjust." This biblical foundation of friendship was a continuation of the Book of Genesis theme that all men are created to "the image and likeness" of God. The second and unique basis for friendship introduced by Christianity was the ideology that, through the instrumentality of baptism, the faithful are granted a higher form of life which is a participation of the God-man Christ's life. This incorporation of all Christians into the "one-body" of Christ makes any act of friendship toward another Christian into an act of friendship to Christ. "There is no longer Jew or Gentile, slave or free, male or female, but we are all one person in Christ Jesus Our Lord." The conception that "all men are brothers," is Christianity's attempt to justify an universal similarity sufficient to enable men to live in peace with one another.

THEORY OF FRIENDSHIP IN MODERN SOCIOLOGY

Modern sociological theory of the last century has been much interested in the classification of human relations, particularly of the various kinds of groups which men create, and of the patterned forms of human relations which dominate these groups. The sociological line of approach is somewhat different from that of Aristotle, who found mutual friendly relations in every form of social grouping, but who classified many of these as less perfect forms of friendship.

The modern sociologists ordinarily use the "ideal method" and attribute primarily to any form of human relation only its unique contribution. For instance, businessmen may also be good friends among themselves, but, according to the post-Comtean sociologists, since the essence of the business relationship is profit, this relationship between the two businessmen is categorized as a "contractual one for profit."

The modern sociologists who have classified social groupings and social relations have been very numerous in nearly all countries and in every decade. A summary by name would be tedious and useless. Hence we avoid all that by taking as outstanding representatives F. Tonnies for Germany, E. Durkheim for France, P. Kropotkin for Russia, M. Ginsberg for England and C. H. Cooley for the United States. The ideas of the others are substantially similar.[1]

Essentially these men tend to divide all social groups into three main categories—(1) *synthetic* and governing ones, such as states and churches; (2) primary ones pervaded by *community*

[1] A summary of most of these is given in E. Dekany, *Communauté et Organizations,* Paris, 1940.

feelings; and (3) secondary ones called *organizations*. In addition to these three "real types" of groups they recognize others of a nominal type such as crowds, agglomerations, and so on, but the three real organizations above are the ones given most analysis.

The primary groups, those of a community nature, are the ones claimed to be most surcharged with feelings of friendship. Here, in a large degree, persons are face to face with one another and have had continued social relations over long periods. During these periods they may not have eaten "salt" together but they at least have had many intimate relations in common because most such experiences—e.g. a new school, snow removal or an epidemic—are community wide.

PRIMARY AND SECONDARY GROUPS

The primary organizations are based very much upon territorial (community) or other close physical relations. This does not mean that contiguity of people in a small area leads to the inclusion of everyone in any one friendship group, but it does mean that friendships arise pretty much because of local territorial proximity. Unless the people who form friendships because they are alike, remain alike, they lose their friendship as Aristotle noted three and a half centuries before the Christian era.

On the other hand, *organizations* are of an *"interest"* nature hence contractual and selective of persons from various territorial and non-contiguous groups. Organizations, or secondary groups, generally include some who are friends and tend to make other friends, but fundamentally the factors leading to what Aristotle called "the highest grade of friendship" are to be found in the community types of organizations, and that kind of friendship is most prevalent there.

For the primary organizations, each sociologist had a term expressing its most characteristic form of social relation. Thus the primary group for Cooley was "face to face"; for Tonnies, it was *gemeinschaft* or "village-like"; for Durkheim it was "mechanical social organization" or one based upon a very enlarged *conscience collective* or group mental agreement in values; for

Kropotkin it was mutual aid groups; and for Ginsberg, it was the *comprehensive* and *enduring* groups such as the family, neighborhood and small community.

The secondary organizations were for Cooley not face-to-face, but rather based upon an assumption of a specific interest; for Tonnies, these were *gesellschaft* or business-like; for Durkheim these were "organic social organizations" with a high development of the individuality *(conscience individualiste);* for Kropotkin these were competitive groups; and for Ginsberg, they included only *limited* and specific forms of human relations.

The important point of this is that all sociologists recognize friendship, and its derivatives or associated social organizations, as *primary,* a major form of *social existence,* as being particularly in the field of *relations surrounding the family* wherein character is formed, and as of being *paramount in all societies.*

In addition it should be pointed out that these sociologists generally imputed character control to the friendship organizations or primary groupings. They of course meant character control insofar as it is not a purely family matter. Not all these sociologists paid particular attention to the family, since it is generally assumed to be a pervasive and constant factor in human relations. Their main concern was with groups outside of the family, somewhat after an earlier main sociological theory from 1500 to 1750 that the family and state were "natural groups" and all others, subject to study by general sociology, man-made groups.[2]

---

[2] In the past fifty years, due partly to the influence of Marxian anti-family propaganda, there has been a movement among family sociologists to classify the family into the category of non-natural groups. This was the fundamental meaning of the fashion for defining the family as "only a unity of interacting personalities" which has stultified much of our family sociological literature since 1930. Since every group of any kind may be defined by these same words, this was an attack upon the natural law conception of the family. However, this movement has not begun to recede rapidly in favor of the "natural theory" of the family again. On this problem see the work, *Genossenschaftsrecht,* by Otto Von Gierke as translated by E. Barker.

INTER-FAMILY FRIENDSHIPS MOST IMPORTANT

This brief study of friendship as considered by the great social thinkers in history points out some of its main social-relations characteristics. Friendship is a form of social interchange of a voluntaristic, non-compulsive nature. It is noted that it thrives best among equals who have face-to-face relations with each other over relatively long periods. Essentially it is something not for profit or gain in an economic sense, although there may be incidental economic increments.

Friendship is not a pleasurable relation in the meaning of the distinct senses or appetites because these wear themselves out quickly by over-saturation. It lasts and must last a long time, even for life. However, the presence of friendship does not prohibit mutual pleasure, especially on the rather low threshold of mere companionship, occasional gain and incidental protection.

Friendship is not essentially a within-family or domestic relation because, except between husband and wife, this is not a meeting or cojoining of equals. Even husband and wife are not "equals" because each has a different role and as such cannot be equated, although their roles must have equal value in family life. There may be, and often is, friendship between parent and child, but that is incidental and subsidiary to the inequality of minds, physique and the differing roles of the old and young. Friendship exists between husband and wife but that is something in addition to the love and sex interests and the differing roles they have to assume in relation to their children.

While friendship is not essentially a domestic relation, it involves the household and family because real intimacy involves inter-family visiting or what the Greeks called the "eating of salt together." In that respect friendship in its essence is a relation between the two family adults of two different families because husband and wife in the same family have more primary relations.

A husband and wife legally and socially have a monopoly right in each other as against the world. Thus real friendship between two men must involve the acceptance of this relation by the wives, and vice versa. While friendship is between groups of family adults, fundamentally, it also involves the children because of the principle or coloration and discoloration. A parent is on a primary social relation with his children and from them he cannot be separated except by the inner-family processes. Relations between parents and children are also, as in the case of husband and wife, a mutual monopoly right, unless specifically *excepted by law or custom.*

"DOMESTIC RELATIONS" ARE NOT PRIMARY FRIENDSHIPS SINCE THEY BECOME COMPULSORY

The placing of domestic relations—those between husband and wife, parent and child, sibling and sibling, spouse and in-law, or grandparent and grandchild—out of the perfect or pure friendship category needs explanation. All these domestic persons may be friends with each other, or with some of the others, and generally are. However, these domestic persons have always had legally defined "rights" against one another. These rights presume obligations, and hence the social relation between domestic persons is not voluntaristic.

A parent has an obligation to support his child and to rear him correctly. He has also the right, inherent in the obligation, to discipline the child. A wife has the right to demand support from her husband and, on the other hand, he has the right, against the "world at large," for her companionship and loyalty—not only to him but also to his children, and even his aged parents in most cases. And *vice versa,* the loyal wife, who assumes her obligations, has similar rights against her husband. A study of inter-family homicide, even in our advanced public courts of today, shows that a woman who kills a disloyal, unfaithful or neglectful husband is seldom punished and nearly always freed on some legal fiction.

Thus domestic relations are ruled out of the category of perfect friendship on two grounds. Domestic social relations are fundamentally "compulsive" and hence only imperfect friendships; and while domestic relations are nearly always friendly, their primary essence is of status, and not of friendship. Fundamentally, friendship relations are neither status-forming in a legal sense, as in the family, nor contractual, as between persons seeking economic gain.

PRIMARY FRIENDSHIPS EXTEND FAMILY RELATIONS

Friends of a family are generally other families. The primary friendly relation is between the adults although children are involved, because an adult is a parent as well as a friend. Thus the inner fringe of friendship is fundamentally the household. The outer fringe is marked by any circumstance which prevents intimacy, from mutual pleasure on a low level, to a deep sharing of basic knowledge of life.

Contiguity of residence, or the ability to achieve it quickly, is more or less a necessity for friendship. Equality in most basic circumstances seems essential. At least inequality must not be a paramount and striking fact. While the inner fringe of friendship is more or less marked off by the domestic doorway, the outer fringe is not far from it. Equality in such a thing as values, which is paramount to friendship, would limit friendships of primary nature to those families with close resemblances.

Friendships of a real primary character cannot be numerous. Aristotle noted this in his remark that "To be a friend to many people, in the way of the perfect friendship, is not possible." Intimacy is the sharing of the individual personality and that is not a very expendable item. Spouses share most with each other but even this sharing is limited. No one knows a person but himself. Sharing between a parent and child is sharply limited by the nature of their relationship. Hence intimacy is limited and intimate friends are not numerous. Sharply limiting intimacy with friends is the fact that primary friendship is among groups (families) and each additional person involved in a friendship can only limit, and not add to the extensivity of the friendship circle.

There are of course many secondary or partial friendships which are relations between individuals. However, these secondary friendships are not as intensive as the primary ones and do not have the social implications of the primary ones.

INDIVIDUAL FRIENDSHIPS ARE SECONDARY

Friendship is a universal form of human relations. The conception here of friendly relations between families as the purest primary type of friendship is not to derogate that between individuals. Rather, it is to point out that the family is the primary unit of society and most persons, unless in a disrupted or artificial state, are family members by status. (This status determines our basic rights and obligations to others, such as citizenship, inheritance, obligations of supporting others or being supported, and so on.)

All persons in a large degree are in relations of mutual *alieni juris* to family members. In other words, they are in deeply involved genetic relations to family members which restrict other social relations. Consequently, families recognize that mutual friendships are an extension of social relations above the basic social bonds and must not run counter to them. A husband, a wife, a parent or a child cannot ordinarily have successful friendships which interfere with or curtail the family dictates and needs.

One of the great weaknesses of most sociological analyses of group life, and its influence upon the individual, is the failure to recognize that artificial, or formed groups, are always an extension of natural or genetic familistic-derived-and-channeled obligations. For instance take the conception "guilt by association." Through his family a person becomes an American. If he associates with an enemy of the state he is held to have done wrong by forming a friendship contrary to family-derived status.

The major function of friendship seems to be the attachment it gives the individual with the outside world. It is a sort of a chain linkage with the world at large. It helps the individual to understand the world at large, and the world at large to understand the individual. The approach of one to the other on most matters of major concern is through friendships.

Furthermore, it is "comfortable" to be with friends and to have primary friendships. Thus a secondary function of friendship is the psychological protection of the individual. Fundamentally this psychological protection of friendship is in the value systems. On major issues friends think alike, and the closer the friendship, the more they think alike.

MEASURES OF FRIENDSHIP DIMENSIONS

From the above analysis we reach the conclusion that friendship must eventually rest upon a similarity of values, of experiences, of aims in life and of general agreement in the total personalities of the friends. So before we can proceed to an analysis of the significance of friendship we have to agree upon measures of these similarities of values, experiences and aims.

For this we establish the following theoretical table which lists the friendship dimensions or factors under five headings— equality, similarity of experiences, testing time, agreeableness and similarity in family ideals. These are names we apply to the five qualities of primary friendship recapitulated above. In Table 49 opposite each dimension of friendship we give empirical measures or primary tests of this characteristic or dimension. Our problem then is limited to find if the family friends in each and all of the cities studied meet these qualifications.

Table 49

THEORETICAL CLASSIFICATION OF
INFLUENCES IN FRIENDSHIP SELECTION

Theoretical Friendship Dimension	*Primary Tests of Use of this Dimension in Kinship Selection*
Equality of Friends	Income groupings same
Similarity of Experiences	Regions of origin same
Testing time (accessibility over years)	Region of origin the same: selection from same neighborhood
Agreeableness of Personalities	Kindred (intermarriage): Income groupings same
Similarity of Family Ideals	Religion same: Same attitudes toward sizes of families

INCOME, REGION OF ORIGIN, RELIGION AND KINDRED

Table 49 suggests that a good measure of equality of friends is the tendency for them to fall more within the same income groupings than chance would have it. A measure is the proportion of their friends within their same income group as opposed to the proportion of friends of all other families in this same group. In Los Angeles, for illustration, the families with incomes less than $2000 a year had 39.4 per cent of their friends with incomes less than $2000 a year. However, as seen in Table 50, all

Table 50

SELECTIVITY OF FRIENDS IN LOS ANGELES
BY SAME INCOME CLASS

Income groups of student families	Per cent of this group's friends in same income class	Per cent of all other groups' friends in this income class	Ratio of selectivity over chance
Less than $2,000	39.4	4.6	8.5
$2,000 to $5,000	59.4	23.7	2.5
$5,000 to $10,000	56.9	29.3	1.9
More than $10,000	44.7	10.4	4.3

other families (those with more than $2000 a year) had only 4.6 per cent of their friends from the "under $2000 group." This means that poor people had poor friends (economically speaking) 8.5 times more than other people had poor friends.

On the opposite side of the income scale, the people with incomes of more than $10,000 a year had 44.7 per cent of their friends with similar high incomes. All families with less than $10,000 a year had only 10.4 per cent of their friends in the $10,000 class. This means that well-to-do families had well-to-do friends 4.3 times more than others.

For the matter of similarity of experiences we have classified region of origin (as explained later) as one good measure of this influence in choice of friendship. Testing time (accessibility over a number of years) may also be measured by region of origin because we know from this and other studies of migration, both internal and overseas, that friends or persons who knew each other in the former domicile tend to get together and continue these associations again in the new area. In addition to region of origin, this factor of testing time (eating the requisite amount of salt together) can be measured also by selection of friends from the same neighborhood.

For the friendship dimension, "agreeableness of personalities," we have suggested kindred as one measure and similarity of income groupings as another. Similarity of blood and inter-marriage are two very determining factors in similarities of personalities.[3] We know from other studies that marriage not only selects persons very much like each other but, if it is successful and continues, it molds into greater likenesses. Then also the inheritance within families of many physical traits having to do with similarities of personalities is now proved.

Similarity of income groupings is also a measure of agreeableness of personalities. Consumption of economic goods, or similarity in standards of living, is a matter of agreeableness long analyzed and studied.

Similarity of family ideals may be measured by selection of friends from the same religious groupings or faiths. Religions have always been concerned with their own peculiar family doctrines.

In a previous chapter we have already shown that kindred plays a dominant role in friendship. Even in our large cities of today friends are kindred in a high percentage of cases and the closer friends are more often kindred than the farther-away friends.

We have also indicated in the previous chapters the importance of selectivity from the same neighborhood and the general tendency for friends to show the same attitudes towards "reproducing families."

---

[3] See Chapter VII, especially footnote four, in Zimmerman-Cervantes, *Marriage and the Family,* Henry Regnery Co., Chicago, 1956, for a full documentation of this.

SAME REGION OF ORIGIN HIGHLY PREFERRED

In the preliminary analysis we noted that region of origin might be a dominant factor in the selection of friendships because of similarity of earlier experiences of the people. This influence may be demonstrated and proved in detail.

Table 51

SELECTIVITY OF FRIENDS IN LOS ANGELES BY REGION OF ORIGIN

Region of origin of parents of seniors	Per cent of this group's friends from this region	Per cent of all other groups' friends from this region	Ratio of same regional preference over chance
Pacific Coast	59.9	29.0	2.1
Rocky Mountains	29.8	6.5	4.6
Midwest	52.8	23.2	2.3
Southwest	34.1	7.9	4.4
South	32.4	6.1	5.3
East	42.5	14.6	2.9
Other countries	30.4	6.4	4.8

The data in Table 51 from Los Angeles show region of origin to be very important in friend selectivity.

Persons born in one region pick friends from twice to five times more frequently from that region than do persons born in other regions.

The median age of the fathers and mothers of our high school seniors is in the neighborhood of forty-five years. American cities, especially in the West, have had their phenomenal growth during this half century. It is therefore highly probable that the parents of our seniors, as well as all others their age, have migrated to that city from some region. The majority of city dwellers of fifty years of age or over are region "tainted" rather than natively "city tainted." In one respect all American cities are more alike than regions are alike. Insofar as a city differs, as, for instance, Catholic Boston from Protestant Los Angeles, the difference is not an urban one but one *in an urban area* because of different regions of origin of the people.

These regional differences are not yet eradicated within the city. In a large sense the "city influence" is the same all over the country if not all over the world. Persons in cities live in closely packed houses, work in factories, have common working hours, eat noon meals at the factories or business establishments, travel by the same systems whether by auto in Los Angeles or by subway in Boston, read the same newspapers, go to the same types of schools with standard texts and have the same forms of recreation.

But regions are different and remain so largely because the factors in a region are tied to geography, climate, settlement, grand historical experiences and other very slowly changing forces or influences. This may be illustrated for the United States by a recital of the common experiences in several such "regions" as the South, the Urban-Northeast and the Pacific. In the South we may point out the long historical experiences of two groups of people living together, visibly different, the Negro and the White. These have to do with slavery, Civil War, reconstruction and now the battle over segregation. Perennially the Southerner has a very conscious regional tradition, one which has embraced within it the traditions of one of the bloodiest wars in history.

TASTES AND TRADITIONS VARY BY REGIONS

The Urban-Northeast also has its own distinct regional traditions. Before the Revolutionary War the territory of this region was largely unsuited for a prosperous agriculture because of the recent glaciated nature of most of its small stony fields. In the American Revolution it turned quickly to manufacturing, since its earlier sailing ship commerce with the West Indies and with Europe was now disrupted, and it manufactured things of cloth, iron and chemicals, which were badly needed. After the Revolution this manufacturing and trading tradition continued, developed and contrasted with the agrarian cotton and slave-plantation tradition of the south.

After 1830 the new immigrants began to come to the Northeast for work in the mills, factories, canals, railroads. These migrants were, from the beginning, very largely Roman Catholic and the widespread Catholic-Protestant religious differences began to develop early.

Long before the Civil War the *Know Nothing* movement had swept throughout the North and the Urban-Northeast in particular. Many states of the region had Senators and Governors of this particular "anti-foreign" party. As the American party in the election of 1856 they had a presidential candidate, Millard Fillmore. This was an anti-Catholic movement. President Fillmore as a *Know Nothing* candidate was not re-elected. Nevertheless, since that time this struggle between Protestants and Catholics has been a dominant regional pattern in the Urban-Northeast and may be spoken of as one of the partial common denominators in the impressment of the common regional value systems.

The Pacific regional value systems, though different in content, are regional in location and also of long continued semipermanent fixation. This is essentially a region made up of migratory interior native-born Protestant Americans who have come recently to the area but are always being overwhelmed by new waves of these same interior native-born Americans. There were but a few hundred English-speaking North Americans in California, for instance, when we took it over from Mexico in 1847. But the discovery of gold in 1848 changed that. In 1849 it was a territory and in 1850 a state of more than 250,000 people, mostly native-born American migrants. From then to now, when the whole Pacific region is growing faster than any other in America, the regional problem has been the same—one of neighbors scarcely acquainted being engulfed by thousands of new migrants each year. We need not further document this well-known fact.

In one of these regions (South) it is color, in another (Urban-Northeast) religion, and in the third (Pacific) the overweening newness and brittleness of human relations that makes dominant "regional patterns."

Knowing this, then, we are not surprised to find "region of origin" as a prominent factor in friendship formation. As in the case of kinship, it seemed that the region must be a factor in "similarity of values, experiences and aims in life." Since the migrant family is primarily on the move because of a man searching for a job, we used the region of origin of the husband or father as the measurable index of that similarity which comes closest to reality.

While we present data for only one city here, the same tables for the six cities show that friends are from the same region of origin more than as if chosen by chance in about similar proportions, as in Los Angeles.

FRIENDS ON THE SAME INCOME LEVEL PREFERRED

In the theoretical analysis it was suggested that similarity by income groupings might be used as a measure of the quality of friends and in the "agreeableness of personalities." The data from Los Angeles show that families do pick friends from the same income class in much greater proportions than random or chance selection would suggest.

All student families were divided into four income levels. Then for the families of each income level we compared the per cent of their friend-families which they had reported in the same income group as themselves with the per cent of friend-families in that class reported by the remainder of the student families. Thus, families with less than $2000 yearly had 39.4 per cent from that class, whereas others had only 4.6 per cent of their friends from this minus $2000 group. This gives a selectivity ratio for families of the same income group of 8.5 times chance. Families also show pronouncedly more economic selection with respect to their closest friends than with respect to others.

The relationship of income to character of the persons receiving and spending those incomes has been one of the most discussed subjects in economic theory. Income getting has been claimed as a measure of standards of tastes and outlook upon life. We do not have to summarize all these theories nor to settle any arguments as to the definitiveness of income as a measure of ability or opportunity or level of living or taste. The bulk of evidence is sufficient for us to proceed to use similarity of income groupings as both a measure of equality of the persons, whether innate or acquired, and the agreeableness of their personalities. In these respects we use income groupings as a measure of homogamy or likeness in friendship selection. The results for Los Angeles are the same as in other cities.

FRIENDS IN THE SAME RELIGION PREFERRED

In our theoretical analysis it was suggested that selection of friends from groups of the same religious faith would be a good measure of the similarity of family ideals of the friend groups. This does not mean that any one religious group has a monopoly on family ideals but rather that different faiths have practices unique to their confessions. For our purposes, in seeking to measure the nature of the "impermeable walls" about the minds of the teen-agers, the similarity of these convictions within the friendship groupings is what we seek. In Table 53 from Los Angeles, we show that families prefer friends in their own faiths from three to thirty times more frequently than chance selection.

The small orthodox groups, Jews, Mormons and most devout Catholics were most selective of friends from the same religious confessions but all groups gave at least a three times greater preference for intimate friends of their own faith.

WHY SIMILAR FRIENDS ARE PREFERRED

In the theoretical analysis we expected some selective relation between primary friendships of parents as a vehicle for the control of the viewpoints and of the motivation of children. The child is not a free agent but stands *alieni juris* or under the wing of his parents. He cannot be freed from this except by specification, as, for instance, by the compulsory school attendance laws of the past one or two generations. What a child sees of life, except as the parental system fails, or as he successfully rebels, is only a partial segment or a carefully expurgated and censored view of the world as a whole. Why this is so we shall not discuss further here except to say that an infant is not an adult and is not ordinarily allowed to act as an adult. The customary and written law of nonage is as old as society itself. In spite of all contentions to the contrary, to wit, that we now live in a world of "individualism," the obligation of parent to child has increased and been strengthened tremendously in American family law of this century.[4]

The ordinary American city, even any neighborhood within it, is composed of persons of varied origin, wealth and religious confession. In order to have any agreement among the intimate friends within a home, these have to be picked selectively.

We may illustrate this by the religious affiliation of the high school seniors' mothers in St. Louis, and of their best family friends, for 1954-55. Among these were 4,176 Protestants, 8,406 Catholics, 582 Jews, 1,686 "others" (mostly Pentecostalites or new "faith" sects) and 306 who were classified as non-believers, or persons who were simply neutral and non-involved with religion or religious institutions. Thus in 15,156 friend-families of high school seniors' mothers, it would be almost impossible, in a social sense, to pick five or six at random and have them of similar values. The Protestants are of all denominations. The Catholics are a mixture of Irish, German, Italian and old American Catholics from the South. The Jews are few. The Pentecostalites even deny that they are Protestants.

The so-called non-believers are only a segment (2 per cent of the total). The problem is further complicated by the fact that some of all these groups, particularly the Protestants and Catholics, are split as to color. St. Louis has a large Negro element. Also St. Louis is a city of importance in a large surrounding area of Missouri, and southern Illinois which is primarily Protestant.

---

[4] The increasing requirement of parent to child in American law is documented in C. G. Vernier, *American Family Laws,* Volume III, *Parent and Child,* Stanford University Press, Palo Alto, California, 1936; White House Conference, *The American Family,* 1948, Chapter VI.

RANDOM CHOICE DIFFERS FROM FAMILY CHOICE OF FRIENDS

In tabular form comparative data on religious affiliation of mothers of the high school seniors and their friends are given in Table 52 for four of our cities.

Table 52

RELIGION OF MOTHERS OF HIGH SCHOOL STUDENTS
IN FOUR CITIES

Faith	Omaha	Denver	Boston	St. Louis
Protestant	3,372	3,210	828	4,176
Catholic	4,158	3,516	5,862	8,406
Jewish	258	162	420	582
Other*	672	420	168	1,686
None	138	192	24	306
Total	8,598	7,500	7,302	15,156

* Pentecostalites, Mormons, Christian Scientists and others.

If a Protestant picked his friends by random chance in the high school circles of Omaha, he is about as liable to get a Catholic as another Protestant. This is also somewhat true for Denver. In St. Louis he has a twice greater chance for picking a Catholic, whereas in Boston, where Protestants are a minority group, he would have to pick eight friends before he could be fairly sure of another Protestant.

Catholics who, as pointed out above, are divided ethnically are in a similar situation. Ethnically is used here in the sense largely of mother tongue, by origin or tradition. In Boston, random picking of friends would almost assure a Catholic getting another of this faith, but the associational cleavages between those of Irish, Italian, French or other origin are as great as between Protestants and Catholics in other cities. The groups of "Jews," "Others," and "None" stand little chance indeed of getting someone like themselves by random choice.

SELECTIVE SIMILAR FRIENDS AND VALUE CONTROL

Our only workable assumption, in a situation such as this, is that the choosing of family friends is highly selective. Teen-agers are thus provided with an existing world which they see and trust. It is peopled by persons whose values are very much like their parents'.

Only in this manner can teen-age motivation according to the ideals of the parents be retained and reinforced. The families the child sees in the home are similar to his own and to each other in fundamental measurable indices of values, such as religion, region of origin, kinship and economic status. We may predicate that the family friendships are a fundamental factor in helping the individual families in their teen-age motivation aims. And if the best families (those having the most success in teen-age control) use this principle more than those of less success, we will have added materially to the proof of our point.

Table 53

SELECTIVITY OF FRIENDS IN LOS ANGELES
BY SIMILAR RELIGION OF FATHER OF FAMILIES

Religion of student families	Per cent of this group's friends in this faith	Per cent of all other groups' friends in this faith	Ratio of selectivity to chance
Protestant	77.1	25.2	3.0
Catholic (in public schools)	37.6	12.0	3.1
Catholic (in parochial schools)	61.4	12.0	5.1
Jewish	60.3	2.0	30.0
Other (Mormons and Christian Scientist)	63.3	7.9	8.0
None (free thinkers)	27.8	6.1	4.5

We do not present data on all cities for all traits because, except for religious affiliation, they are all about the same. In the trait of religion (Table 54) we see some characteristic general patterns. The high orthodox (like the Jews) stand first as to

Table 54

FRIENDSHIP SELECTIVITY BY RELIGIOUS CONFESSION IN FIVE CITIES

Religion	Boston	New Orleans	St. Louis	Denver	Omaha
Protestant	6.0	3.7	5.7	5.1	4.9
Catholic	3.3	1.5	5.0	5.2	4.0
Jewish	42.1	***	55.0	46.6	47.8
Other*	56.0	5.4	15.7	14.3	12.1
None	**	8.3	4.9	6.6	6.6

* "Other religions" are a varied group differing much among themselves. We believe them to be mainly Christian Scientists in Boston, Pentacostalites in St. Louis and Mormons in the Western cities.

** Only four families in Boston claimed no religious confession. They had nineteen friends in the "others" group.

***No Jewish graduates were reported from the New Orleans' school studied.

psychosocial isolation of themselves. The unusual other orthodox groups (Mormons, Christian Scientists and Pentecostalites) stand second. This explains why the minority of Protestants in Boston are more selective than Catholics, whereas in Los Angeles the minority Catholic segment is more selective than Protestants.

A child will usually begin by accepting his parental value systems. If he retains these values through his teens, the family has won its battle. Thus in the good families he completes high school, if he is adequately competent to do so. If his family adult friends have the same values as he sees in his parents, his basic ideas are not challenged. If our hypothesis is true, as our evidence seems clearly to indicate, it raises some fundamental principles for sociological theory.

SUMMARY AND ANALYSIS

This chapter surveys the historical thinking of Western society as to the nature and significance of friendship as a form of human relations. The analysis leads to the conclusion that *friendship between similar minded adults living in proximity over a period of years results in its most basic or primary type.* The friendship of this type is between equals, is voluntaristic, involves common experiences and is not primarily for appetitive pleasure or political, economic or social gain.

This type of friendship is in accord with and an addition to family relations since familism is a legal monopoly of members allowing only clearly specified intrusions upon and releases to its members. *Semper praesumitur pro matrimonio* (the presumption is always in favor of marriage or the family) is an old legal phrase which summarizes this nature of the family. Consequently, friendship between parents, giving outsiders only limited access to domestic situations, makes a world for children, because they see their parents in their parental friends and *vice versa.* This is the "envelope" of the teen-ager, from which he is gradually released for educational purposes and for preparation for a life in the world on his own.

FRIENDSHIP SIMILARITY AND TEEN-AGE MOTIVATION

Theoretical analysis indicates that these parental friendships have to be highly selective because voluntaristic friendships can last only if the tastes and values of the friends are the same in essentials and remain so over a number of years. An empirical analysis of about thirty-nine thousand families of high school seniors and their friends in four great American cities shows such diversity of background that it is impossible for them to have similarity of tastes and values if the friends are picked upon a random basis. The way is prepared for the testing of the selectivity of friendship. The hypothesis is that control of teen-age motivation is achieved through the similarity of values (psychological security) represented in these friendship groups.

Historically the family system, with its fringe components of kindred and "clients" (non-related friends), has been a protective organization. In the absence of highly developed governments two forms of this protection have been recognized in all Western law customs and codes. One of these is called "passive social solidarity" in legal sociology and the other "active." Under passive social solidarity the kindred and clients protected the family and its members from harmful intrusion. Active solidarity sought justice and restitution for damages done by outsiders to the family members. These are two forms of protection, prevention and reprisal.

With the development of modern police, certain limited forms of obvious protection have passed into the hands of the agents of the public at large. However, the family as a "natural" and legally prescribed way of life only yields its functions, powers, duties and rights as specified, retaining all others, which are multitudinous in scope.

Psychological protection of members and motivation of the children has not been invaded by the public, and it scarcely seems possible that these would be given up by the family. As a matter of fact the trend in all our modern courts is in reverse of this. The definition of a good parent and his duties to his children has become increasingly rigid and complicated. Nonage which could be abrogated mutually at twelve for females and fourteen for males during the Western middles ages has moved up in years. "Age of consent" is now at least sixteen for females; "Age of free consent" eighteen; compulsory school laws are almost as high. Voluntaristic nonage, in which parents are expected to see children through college and professional schools, has mounted rapidly to about twenty-five years of age.

This study of psychological protection and motivation of the children through this vastly extended (doubled) nonage is very much helped by selective friendships of families. We have measured this by kinship, neighborhoods of residence, regions of origin, economic standing and religious faiths.

THE VIRILITY OF THE
AMERICAN FAMILY SYSTEM

chapter **XII**   THIS BOOK IS BOTH PRACTICAL AND THEORETICAL.
We seek to show how successful American families become so. That is the practical problem. We desire some insight into the longevity of our American culture, insofar as this is determined by family behavior. That is our basic theoretical problem.

One of the favorite attacks upon our country by Communist agitators in other lands is that we are dissolute and "family decadent." They use four arguments which they pick up from our "slick" magazines. One, high divorce; two, frequent juvenile delinquency; three, our women have most of the money and the power; and four, the degenerating males have turned to psychiatrists because they have no role to play and are becoming homosexual.

There are good answers to all these claims. High divorce and juvenile delinquency rates may both be explained by the polarization thesis elaborated in this book. Women do possess most of the money wealth in the United States. This is due to the fact that our women outlive our men by about ten years. With high taxes and the expenses of families, men cannot save much money in their lifetimes. They purchase insurance and annuities and have pensions for their own old age and that of their wives. Then they die off and the money goes to their widows. The money is then in savings banks and in trust funds where it is nearly always managed by men. After thirty-five, every age class has a high preponderance of females and these are the ones who have inherited the wealth from their husbands. Finally, the major reason for the American urban male's recourse to the psychiatrist is the stress, tension and competition arising from overwork. Homosexuality is a crime in this country and its incidence is reported and talked about. In many other countries it is not a legal offense and it is taken for granted. Sensational stories about these deviant sexual activities published in our popular magazines, without careful analysis, substantially harm us in the eyes of the world.

IMPORTANCE OF CULTURAL LONGEVITY

The problem of the longevity of a cultural system, such as that of a world power like the United States, is of extreme importance in theoretical sociology as well as in practical affairs. Any cultural composition, such as a national state, has to serve some worthwhile purposes in order to exist over any great period. By serving some worth-while purpose it wins and holds allegiance internally from its own people and externally from others. These allegiances and votes of confidence help it to continue to exist.

One such service of a world power is that it regularizes human relations over wide geographic areas and in many important fields of conduct. Hence many millions of persons begin to depend upon the world power for stability in gaining their livelihoods. They feel that the national power guarantees security in world relations. Hence they give their attention more fully to economic and other cultural pursuits and the areas affected by the influence of the power prosper economically and socially.

We may illustrate this by the general prosperity in the Mediterranean world during the first three centuries of the Christian era when the Roman world state was at its high peak. Commerce and trade flourished. Roads were built and the seas were safe for navigation. Economic production in all the border countries grew because wheat and grain could be produced and shipped to urban centers. Populations, wealth and standards of living increased. Gracious buildings, remains of many of which are still standing, were erected throughout the Roman and its dependent worlds. Considerable evidence indicates that probably never before, and for a long time after, had so many of mankind had such favorable economic and social conditions.

After the breaking of this cultural composition in the fourth and fifth centuries of our era, conditions tended to reverse themselves. Although the Byzantine culture around Constantinople (Istanbul) staved off extreme conditions in that area, the western part of Europe soon fell into chaos and ruin. During the Western dark age from the sixth to the tenth centuries that part of Europe gave way to hunger, cannibalism and starvation. Here where once Europe had been prosperous, highly populated and great, only a few scattered and miserable peasants and fellaheen were left.

ILLUSTRATIONS OF CULTURAL STABILITY AND PROSPERITY

During the next dark period of the West (from A.D. 600 to A.D. 1000) the Arabic-Islamic culture rose to flower and fruit in the Middle East. Then again that eastern part of the older Roman Empire had a new day of revived commerce, peace and prosperity. All this was due largely, it seems, to the benign influence of order and security in basic human relations established by the Arabs and the Byzantines.[1]

The story of the rise and fall of one world power as told here could be repeated for other great cultures as illustrated by Mayan-Aztecan empire in Central America or the Mon-Khymer in Southeast Asia. Previous to these empires, only peasantry with limited livelihoods existed in the areas. During the flowering of these two empires, men there accomplished great things as evidenced by the ruins of the cities in both areas. These are still to be seen. The large area in Central America dominated by the city state federation (Copan, Chichen Itza, Uzmal, Capmeche and Mayapan and later the Aztecan cities) was a unified beehive of prosperity, well-being and industry. All the general region of Southeast Asia which comprises the area south of China and east of India, including the Malay States and parts of Indonesia, was equally prosperous during the height of the Mon-Khymer Empire.

After the Mon-Khymer and Mayan empires fell their areas

---

[1] See an excellent resume in Carleton S. Coon, *Caravan, The Story of the Middle East,* Harper and Brothers, New York 1951, Chapters VI *et passim.*

also suffered a similar poverty-stricken fate for a time, as did western Europe during its dark age after Rome.

The three illustrations of Rome, Mon-Khymer and Mayan, to which many others could be added, are merely to point out the social significance of the longevity of cultures. They emphasize the high importance of the study of basic social change in the field of human affairs. Much, if not most, of the known habitable world is now covered with the ruins of great cultures which once flourished and have decayed.

This fragility of world powers, and their disastrous decay, leads to a discussion of the present family system of the United States of America. It is an attempt to probe a little into what may be signs of cultural longevity within the North American culture.

The family system in the United States is scrutinized because this is believed to have a causal relation with cultural longevity and hence economic and social prosperity.[2]

THE FAMILY SYSTEM AND CULTURAL LONGEVITY

Considerable evidence exists, at least for Western society, that the family system with its changes is closely related to "cultural longevity." In an earlier work, *Family and Civilization,* Zimmerman summarizes this relation for the west from 1500 B.C. down to the present time.[3] While he is presently unwilling to extend these conclusions to the other "worlds" outside of the west because they have not been studied carefully from this point of view, he does believe that such is partly the case generally.

From sources about the non-European worlds, now translated into European languages, it appears that much of the same family-civilization relations have existed among all peoples. However,

---

[2] It is not known who first analyzed the idea of the relation between a cultural system and a "social prosperity" but it certainly was a basic tenet of the sociology of Frederic Le Play in the nineteenth century. For Le Play's ideas see Carle C. Zimmerman and M. E. Frampton, *Family and Society,* D. Van Nostrand Co., New York, 1935, Chapter V.

[3] Harper and Brothers, New York, 1947. Chapter XXIV deals specifically with the family and rhythms in Western Civilization.

that is merely a hypothesis.

A brief summary of the family-civilization thesis for the Western world is as follows. Basically all simple cultures have about the same types of family system: Husband and wife, parents and children. These elements of the nuclear family are found in simple cultures to be dominated in their public relations by kindred, clan and gens groups. Public law of the family-regulation does not exist, except in the common laws of mores and custom. This common law of mores and custom concerns the model types of relations between the elements of the nuclear family. It regulates the steps the kin groups should take to enforce these nuclear mores and to protect the nuclear families and their elements from the outside world.

Simple peoples, as discussed in the above paragraph, include both primitives who have never been active in the greater civilizations and those remnant members of the greater world cultures which have decayed and fallen into oblivion. This kindred rule of the family system prevailed in the West both before Greece and Rome rose to flower and after their decay.[4]

---

[4] For many years Zimmerman has been interested in a study of the conditions of "peasants." He is convinced from a study of the ruins among which most of them exist today that they are in a "resting stage" between greater cultures. Or, at least, they were once enrolled as active members in great cultures now dissipated. If one travels to Yucatan or Siam and Cambodia, he is always studying poverty-stricken peasants nearby to some great ruins. These vestigial remains are gaunt reminders that the present peoples are the impoverished and ignorant progeny of an illustrious and prodigal past. The same is true for Italy, Egypt, North Africa, the Arabic lands, India and China. Oswald Spengler's concept of the "fellaheen" (as the simple timeless peasant between cultures) applies to most of the people in all of North Africa and the Near East. Down the river towards the Mediterranean from Baalbeck in Lebanon is found a whole string of ancient ruins. The areas around these ruins are now cultivated by simple peasants who have no idea what these ruins mean. A description of simpler peoples (primitives) who have not been enrolled in the greater civilizations of the past is given by L. T. Hobhouse, G. C. Wheeler and M. Ginsberg, *The Material Culture and Social Institutions of Simpler Peoples,* Chapman and Hall, Ltd., London, 1915. Simple cultures of the type they describe, however, are not *fellaheen.*

THE CIVILIZED FAMILY SYSTEMS

A second stage in the family-civilization hypothesis for the higher cultures shows that they substitute public law codes representing state power for the legal right of the clans and the gens to control the nuclear family. The public marriage law (Greek law, Roman law, canon law, modern marriage law) then begins to define what is marriage, what is a family, and what are the basic rights and duties of the elements of the nuclear family to each other. Finally, but most importantly, public law ousts the kindred from legal control of the nuclear family.

This second stage, necessary for the growth of trade and communication and development of "public life," is associated with the periods when the great cultures begin to bloom. Between the twelfth and fifteenth centuries, or roughly between the Renaissance and the Reformation, family law was put under public rule. In these centuries the modern Western culture made its important initial gains leading to our present greatness.

The third stage arises when the civilization begins to flower. At this time the individual within the nuclear family, now already freed from kindred and gens domination, begins to receive an increased private right in the handling of his domestic affairs. "Atomization" of society starts. We mark this now in our conversation when we speak of the older family—of a century or so ago—as having been "Victorian." Now it is more individualized.

In this third stage the conditions of freedom and restraint of the individual become about evenly balanced. Decisions on marriages, divorces and the production of offspring are left to individual choice with only informal guidance by religious doctrines and wishes of kindred. However, once a marriage or family choice is made by the individual, public law tries to determine the course and the after effects of these decisions. In such a society an adult man and a woman who are not incestuously related, generally are allowed to marry by choice. Once married they may live about as they wish, *except* in prohibited ways, and within the broad specifications of the mutual rights of the marriage monopoly. They are not required to have children, but if they do so, then the voluminous parent-child law takes over and specifies fairly rigid lines of conduct between parent and child. Divorce or separation is available but it is a legal course involving public law. The marriage is guarded meticulously by the agents of the public, especially where divorce is contested by a non-agreeing spouse, or where children are involved in the marriage.

FRAGILITY OF THE CIVILIZED FAMILY SYSTEM

This highest form of marriage—in a sense that freedom and restraint are about equally balanced—has two social or cultural characteristics. First, it allows the freedom necessary to a highly creative society of rapid change. Second, it leaves the family very much on its own. One of the negative consequences of this freedom will be that its members will be at liberty, if they so choose, to wreck their families and their lives. These kinds of families and societies develop high divorce and desertion rates. Child neglect and juvenile delinquency become common. Family life at any time is so confining that it often causes friction of one kind or another between spouses or parents and children. In the kin-dominated family the relatives act as a go-between and settle these matters. But this public-law-atomized family described above is one which can have very high incidence of breakage.

In the highly civilized cultures with their atomistic families we find the most serious problems of the relation between family breakage and cultural longevity. Civilized societies can develop the "fashion" of holding marriage very lightly. This causes confusion in the culture. Disruption of marriages by numerous divorces leaves thousands of children semi-orphans to be reared by abandoned and helpless mothers or step-parents. Finally, the problem of too few children can arise. An average family of two children, for instance, creates great problems of class, social and cultural survival. Any one of these "shortages of familism" tends to breed other social pathologies. Where divorce is fashionable, childlessness and juvenile delinquency become common. Then the culture may no longer be able to carry out its world mission.

FAMILY SYSTEM DECAY NOT NECESSARY

However, it does not appear that mass family failure and culture dissolution is necessary or inevitable. Such social decay is possible and has happened before in history. This possibility and measures for meeting it influence our present thinking.

The historian Polybius (c. 200 B.C.) speculated on the cause of the decay of the Greece of his era. He pointed to the presence of many relatively childless families. Earlier, such Greek writers as Aristophanes had singled out the decay of reverence for marriage and family vows among all classes of Greece. In the Roman culture, which succeeded that of Greece, the rise to extreme popularity of a very loose form of marriage known as the *"concubinatus"* started its family system toward decay. The Christian reforms after the fourth century A.D. specified the grave problems arising from the neglect of wives and children. The Christian writers (Basil, Jerome, Augustine, Salvian) attributed Roman decay to the widespread family neglect. Zosimus, the non-Christian historian, said the same, but blamed the monks for the trouble. Christian reforms, finally made legal in the fourth part of the Corpus Juris Code (525 to 550 A.D.), sought to reorganize the family system so as to eliminate this neglect of domestic responsibility.

Once again, in our own rendezvous with history, the Euro-American world is plagued with high divorce and desertion rates, millions of resulting semi-orphaned children and the consequent growing juvenile crime rates. In the earlier part of this century the one and two child families became the fashion. The remainder of this chapter examines the family-civilization problem for the United States of today. Is our family system decaying or is it not?

POSSIBLE "CAUSES" OF HIGH RATE OF FAMILY BREAKAGE IN THE U.S.A.

The signs of decay in the family system of America today could be the result of other "causes" than the Spenglerian doctrine of inevitable decay and decline after the flowering of a culture. For instance, the newness of a country such as the United States of America could be the major factor in a short-term period of family confusion.

Our country is not like Mexico which had a strong and highly civilized native population when the Europeans first came to the Americas. In that country the Europeans merely destroyed the older ruling classes and took over. The basis of the family and population there still is Indian. Consequently in Mexico only one basic conflict of values was added by the conquest—that of the Spanish-speaking upper class and the non-Spanish-speaking mass of the people. But in the United States the Indians (about two million settled very thinly) were killed off or removed, and the whole settlement was a new one mainly from Europe and Africa. This cultural conflict in the United States, where people of different ethnic origin live in nearly every small community, could be the major cause of the present confusion in family values.

EUROPEAN THEORIES ABOUT OUR FAMILY SYSTEM

About twenty years ago some European remarked that the "United States had become decadent before it had become civilized." By this he probably meant that we had developed a very fragile family system unusually early in the course of our culture. Our blooming period might be very short contrasted with other cultures of continued strong familism and longer ascendancy. Following out this line of thought, we might say that our country earlier developed a very fragile family system in its isolated days. Later, facing the challenge of its duties as a world power, it had changed and attempted to strengthen its family system. That being the case, our family system could be moving differently now from what it was in the first third of this century. If so, the high indices of family breakage now apparent, might be merely a false façade over a strong structure of resurgent familism. Thus family breakage now would be a hangover from a blundering course of our culture in the late nineteenth century.

Another explanation for our high incidence of family troubles is that the modern world with its compact, interdependent, strident living, its rapid transportation and communication, inevitably precipitates a higher incidence of the breaking of human institutions like the family. In that case, coupled with the fact that we are far advanced in the Atomic and Space Age, we could well expect the contemporary rates of family breakage.

THE FOUR HYPOTHESES

Thus we have four alternative hypotheses for the explanation of the high incidence of family breakage in the United States. The first is the typical theory of growth and decay of a social system much popularized by the Spenglerian "decline of the west" idea. Second, our problem may be due to the confusion arising out of rapid settlement of the country by peoples of different backgrounds. According to this theory, when the "melting pot" has had time to homogenize our culture, we will emerge with a strengthened family system. Third, the idea of polarization. We started with a weakened family system due to the confusion and anonymity of the rapid settlement of a new country. We now wake up to find ourselves a world power with two conflicting currents in the domestic institution. One is the residue of the older fragile institution, still giving its harvest of breakage, and the other is the new movement towards a strengthened family system needed for a world power. Finally, there is the possibility that the nature of modern life makes probable a greater obsolescence of all social institutions, including the individual families.

We do not deny the high divorce, desertion and juvenile delinquent rates in the country. We seek to ascertain whether there are also an increasing number of strong families. Out of this combined analysis we seek a reassessment of the basic forces in the cultural longevity of the country.

IMPLICATIONS OF THE PRESENT STUDY

The study given in the preceding chapters indicates that the American family system is polarizing to the two extremes: many broken families and many more very good ones. In the center are the ordinary every day type—neither broken nor particularly creative. The bad families seem to be getting worse and the good families are increasing and getting better.

What bearing do these results have upon our four basic hypotheses concerning the explanation of these changes?

If there is an inevitable Spenglerian growth and decline principle in civilizations, that decline has not as yet gained great foothold in, or mastery over, the American family system. This is a tentative conclusion from the study.

It could be that the earlier confusion of the family system within the United States was the result, at least in part, of the rapidity of settlement of the country by diverse ethnic and national groups. Since the values and standards of life of each group, even the languages spoken at first, were different, we could expect to find considerable differences of values. These would affect family standards. During this twentieth century the great bulk of our population has become "native-born." Thus, our culture could be homogenizing as of now, and in answer to the "challenge" of world leadership, be creating a new and much stronger family system.

The United States was a small nation of less than 12½ millions in 1830. By 1930 it was about 123 millions but a net 40 millions of persons had migrated here chiefly from Europe in the meantime. We had not melted together. From 1830 to 1930 was a "nominalist period" in our national composition. Our borders held us together but we were not one people.

As of 1959, the country has about 178 millions of persons, a gain of about 56 millions in the past three decades. But that gain is due to many more than 56 million births because the native-born population has replaced all deaths during that period plus making the addition. Thus, most of our people are now "United Statesers" by birth.

We are now in a "realist" period in the American population since nearly everyone is native-born to the soil. The word "realist" is used here in the sense that cultures tend to become "logically-meaningfully integrated." From this point of view, the years 1830 and 1950 are alike in that these separated years are the ones in which most of the American population was native-born. Between these dates are 120 years, or twelve decades, in which the American people always had among them a great mass of undigested newcomers. It began with the Irish famine and the German Revolution of the 1840's, and ended with the rush to our borders after 1918. So we are willing to accept the "challenge theory" of change within our family system as apparently a reasonable partial explanation of the turn toward familism.

THE STRUGGLE BETWEEN GOOD AND BAD FAMILIES

The third theory is that of polarization. When any cultural system tends to move one way, and then slowly turns and moves another, it is reasonable to believe that opposite currents or eddies would develop. Some persons continue the older way and some go the newer. The polarization thesis does not conflict with the earlier idea of movement from nominalism toward realism in the integration of American culture. As a matter of fact, it supplements that thesis and explains why we can have so many broken families and at the same time so many creative ones.

This leads then to the idea of increased rates of obsolescence of personal character in any culture which is highly urban. There the people live close together and strive more urgently toward greater economic and social productivity. Greater personality problems could result. The homogenic cultures of Europe which are now striving very strongly toward higher productive goals also have had increases in their rates of desertions, divorces, quasi-desertions (from alimony and support payments) and juvenile crimes.

CONCLUSIONS

This terse report covers a very large field. It examines the American family system and finds that it has a high rate for breakage and also a high rate for cultural creativity. It suggests that the situation is due partly to historical circumstances. The rapid growth of the country from an assemblage of new im-migrants to a native-born populace meeting the challenge of world power would bring about the diversity.

It seems that the Spenglerian note of inevitable quick decay of our culture is not true as yet. When the family is growing more sound basically the culture can surmount and overcome great difficulties. This was one of the basic ideas of Frederic Le Play.

From another point of view, that of Toynbee, cultures decay when response is inadequate to challenge. Our conclusions in this matter are also optimistic. Insofar as the strengthening of the family in all levels is an adequate response to the challenge of the atomic age, the country seems fundamentally sound.

Finally, our data show this creativity of the family system has been based upon two major premises of importance to sociology —the use of an idea and also of a form of social organization to promote that idea. The idea is to produce a new type of highly literate man adequate for the new civilization. The social or-ganization is the new form of kindred-friend groups used to bolster the nuclear families.

THE CHANGING COURSE
OF THE AMERICAN FAMILY

chapter XIII   IN THIS FINAL CHAPTER THE FULL MEANING O
the study may be discussed. Details are now pu
aside and the more profound aspects are emphasized: (1) Th
study abandons the current engrossment with the pathologica
aspects of social life and emphasizes the good, the wholesome and
the successful families; (2) It goes beyond the contemporar
operational existentialism of most sociological studies and look
at the problem of motivation and social change; (3) It detect
a reversal of movement within the American family system.

For some decades at the first of the century the family in thi
country, as well as in some others, was losing ground, moving
more and more away from its foundations towards individualism
or what the philosophers call nominalism. In recent years there
has been a reversal of this trend in the United States and i
some other countries. The evidence in our study confirms this
reversal of trend.

THE LACK OF BALANCE IN CONTEMPORARY SOCIOLOGY

Sociology, or systematic thinking about human society, i
about twenty-five hundred years old. Since its early beginning
among the Greeks it has speculated about all types of human
events according to what has been considered important at the
time. In the last half century sociology has become increasingly
obsessed with the pathological aspects of life to the relative
neglect of the normal and successful social actions. The following
analysis seeks to show a great present need for paying more
attention to what might be called, in simple language, "good"
or "normal" human behavior. This is necessary because of the
peculiar nature of social change in this century.

At all times social thinkers pay some attention to the abnormal aspects of life. Generally these distressing aspects are mixed with balanced considerations of the normal course of action. As illustrations we may take Dante (1265-1321) and Machiavelli (1469-1527) for an earlier period; August Comte (1798-1857) and Herbert Spencer (1820-1903) for a later one. All four of these writers were deeply concerned about pathological social situations. All four described some of the difficulties of their times but all four tried in one way or another to find remedies.

Each of the four was the major writer on "sociology" for his own particular period in Western society. Two of them, Dante and Machiavelli, were imprisoned, tried and banished for their views on the issues of their day. The third, Comte, was born shortly after the Terror in France and lived throughout the Napoleonic years before taking up active writing in sociological matters. The fourth, Spencer, began his interest in a wide analysis of social affairs four years after Marx had produced the *Communist Manifesto* (1848) and was still writing about them in 1892, forty years later.

All of these writers lived through profound periods of difficulty in Western society and all of them, while paying attention to the abnormal, sought ways and means for its relief. They tried to present a doctrine for the eventual solution of social difficulties by a development in the normal processes in society. All of them predicated the rise of latent resources for leadership in their current situations. They were "balanced" men.

RISE OF PATHOLOGICAL SOCIOLOGY

In our century, however, this balanced approach to sociology has suffered very much from neglect. On the philosophical side we note a best seller has been made of the solutionless pessimism of Oswald Spengler in his *Decline of the West*. This book, which predicts the total decay of Western society in the next century or so, has little of a constructive nature. If Spengler is right, there is no solution. He implies that the quest for cultural immortality is not only hopeless but "continuity of history" is really only a delusion.

We also have books of lesser renown, but certainly claiming hundreds of thousands of readers. Philip Wylie's *Generation of Vipers* offers no solution because, according to this author, our whole generation is branded with a mark of Cain.

In Europe we see the rise to extreme popularity of the existentialist philosophy most often associated with the name of Jean-Paul Sartre. No matter what Sartre may do himself in his plays and in his adhesion to good social "causes," these acts are contrary to his own philosophy. We cannot overlook the fact that existentialism is not only "amoral" but also "immoral." Not only that but it is silly, illogical and not true. It denies the right of a "moral" citizen to have any understanding or normative convictions. According to this brand of existentialism in order to understand a given course, one has to choose such an existence and to live it. Having lived it, one has made a choice and cannot criticize it. Consequently, Simone de Beauvoir, the chief woman writer on existentialism, in her book *The Second Sex* reaches the conclusion that the whole female sex is lacking in hope, is in a treadmill of futility, and is in the "sad fate to be required without respite to repel an enemy instead of working toward positive ends."

We have in America the Kinsey reports which are obsessed with non-familial sexual athleticism. These imply throughout that the whole structure of sexual inhibitions, their control and channeling, is not only unfair, unenforced, unenforceable, inhuman, but also against our "mammalian rights." In other words the Kinsey group implies that sex restrictions should be abolished.

Not only in these better known writers but in our obscure authors as well as in our men of affairs, do we witness a profound lethargy in social creativity. What succeeds is thereby right even though its success brings greater trouble. Appeasement to them is a great virtue even though it is a harbinger of greater vice.

WHY PESSIMISM IN THE TWENTIETH CENTURY?

A number of reasons may be suggested for the twentieth century absorption in the abnormal, the dissolute and the pessimistic.

ome claim that it is the fad or fashion. In earlier centuries books
bout cities, for instance, were works called encomiums or praises.
he title of a recent book on cities is purely cynical—"Our Fair
ity." Now we have turned, in the fashion of our era, to speak
f misery. This is a fashion, it is held, as in the eighteenth cen-
ury it was a fashion to speak always of primitive states of nature
s wonderful.

Two criticisms may be leveled against this argument. One
, that the use of the terms fad or fashion as an explanation for
ur current obsession with pathology is a tautology. To say that
e do a thing because it is a fad is merely to say we do it. The
econd is that the state-of-nature worship device of the time of
ousseau, while it may have been so common as to be a fad,
as also, in its basic use, a social change device. It was a tool
or the reappraisal of the route of man. It was a sort of psycho-
ogical preparation for the linear evolutionary theories of social
hange in the nineteenth century. It made men amenable to the
stronomical changes in life which came about in that century of
he industrial revolution.[1]

In addition, the nature worship device of the eighteenth cen-
ury was also preceded by similar ideological developments. The
redecessors in social change of the seventeenth century had
urned man away from history, as, for instance, the social con-
ract theories of Hobbes and Locke, so that to proceed in the
ighteenth century we had to create new precepts of origin and
irection. So *fad* or *fashion* is not satisfactory as an explanation
f our current pathological obsession.

A second explanation of the pessimism of the twentieth cen-
ury is the claim that we are really more dissolute now than in
revious eras. That, however, cannot be proved. Even if it is
roved, the need for normal solutions is greater. Good and bad
xist simultaneously at all times. Many eras have their bad, such
s the decay of the Roman Empire, rise of the dark age, the

---

[1] See P. A. Sorokin, *Fads and Foibles in Modern Sociology,* Henry
Regnery Co., Chicago, 1956, for an elaboration of the current state of
sociology.

decay of feudalism, the early modern religious wars or the terrib
circumstances in the early factories at the time of Marx an
Engels. The assumption that private action in our age is mud
more dissolute than in others is not provable.

This does not deny that typical moral character varies fro
time to time and that our present culture is one of such inten:
strain upon the individual that it leads to many breakdown
Erasmus wrote a *Praise of Folly* in 1511 in which he maintaine
people were naturally good. He maintained that if some of th
public regulation of life were relaxed the people would be bett
off than under the bureaucratic system current in that centur
This evaluation possibly could not be applied as truthfully to ou
own day. But even in our times we have blamed Fascism an
Communism for the degeneration of the peoples under their rul

Nevertheless, if we match our so-called "bad" deeds wit
our "good" deeds, we could hardly call this a totally degenerat
period. We do live closer together, have more mobility of persor
and more chances for abnormals to create disturbances. We als
hear more about deviances and problems in the press and on th
radio and television.

OUR CONTEMPORARY SOCIAL CHANGE

Without discussing more explanations of our current pathc
logical pessimism in sociology let us turn at once to an explana
tory theory in terms of the mechanism of social change. History
as well as contemporary events, seems to show that broad change
in the collective mind are predecessors to and accompaniments c
great movements from one era to another. We may demonstrat
this by two observed facts. One is that a great change in cor
temporary life is always associated with a profound growth i
disrespect for the older institutions which need to be renovatec
When social classes which represent institutions become object
of scorn, then those institutions must make profound changes

PATHOLOGY AND SOCIAL POLARIZATION

We feel that the grand pessimism of the twentieth century i
an experience similar to others which marked the decay of an ol

nd the advent of a new era. That is, as the Renaissance closed
ie dark age and the Reformation the medieval one, this present
eriod closes the era of the seventeenth to the twentieth centuries
nd marks the beginning of a new period. This new period will
iffer substantially from the older era. Newtonian social physics,
.ucretian or "nature" religion and non-historical views on social
hange must pass. We need new hypotheses on social change and
ie nature of society.

These will require a large-scale reorientation of the values of
ien.

If this be the case, the current pessimism is a reflection of
hat "polarization" of major social values which is necessary in a
eriod of grand change from one era to another. "Polarization
»f values" means that each field of social life will split sharply
»etween those who are socially adequate for a new era and those
vho are inadequate to meet the changing situations. The in-
idequate ideas are disintegrated remnants of the dying era, carry-
ng on their moribund existence even though they have exhausted
heir creativity. These vestigial ideas or outworn values are now
:ausing increasing turmoil in the social atmosphere. The adequate
nterests are those of the forward-looking groups. They cluster
ncreasingly to the opposite pole from the inadequate exhausted
values.

If this explanation of our current pessimism and embroilment
vith pathological social phenomena is true, then now is the time
or persons of discernment to pay much more attention to posi-
:ive social actions. We need to stress the abilities which help
»ersons to bridge the gap from one era to another. We are not
;oing to find the solution to the problems of the new and coming
:ra by increasingly wallowing in the mire created by the outdated
»ld.

This is a theory of social change which moves out of gradual-
ism and transformationalism. It moves from pessimism to a new
positivism. Even now we cannot explain to our children how we
used to live in 1900-1915. Apparently our children will have as
much difficulty telling their children how they live now. This be-

ing the case, it is imperative for us to look for successful adapta
tions to the newer era.

This idea that the middle half of the twentieth century is one
of a grand transition explains our current pathological sociology
as arising from the differentiation between two classes of persons
There are those making themselves adequate for the new world
which is forming and those failing to change. Since on the whole
it seems that the present family adjustment is proceeding at a
civilization-adequate rate, it behooves us to study the newly
adjusted.

To put this concretely, a minority segment of our population
seems to be manufacturing most of our pathologies. The great
majority are trying for socially-adequate actions such as strong
families and educated, moral children. Our pathologies are largely
cumulative actions in a minority. Divorce, desertion, quasi-
desertion, juvenile delinquency, use of narcotics and the other
pathologies studied by our sociologists are very much concentrated within the same groups of families.

NATURE OF SOCIAL CHANGE IN OUR CENTURY

That social change in the twentieth century is ushering in a
new era needs explaining and stressing. We can look back on
our history and see that vast social change is episodic. In each
grand segment of time there have been periods of several centuries very much alike but these have been interspersed between
"critical periods" in which the eras changed from one to another.
A figure of speech expressing it best might be that of changing
tempo in a relay race. Once a given runner has finished his preliminary spurt he settles down to a steady pace. Then when he
approaches his successor, he spurts again, then hands the mark
on. The fresh runner then tries to gain rank.

Our modern society took off with the plethora of basic in-
ventions and ideas, including the pure Newtonian mechanistic
view of the world, all of which had arisen in the circumstances of
the sixteenth century. From then on till the twentieth we moved
gradually toward the realization of those ideas. But in this twen-

tieth century we repeat something of a grand break similar to the experience of the sixteenth. We have discovered and are assimilating a brand new set of ideas which supersede many of those of the sixteenth. Thus the twentieth century in this respect is more like the sixteenth than like the eighteenth or nineteenth.

This twentieth century change process has produced an entirely new class of people, neither rural nor urban. They live in the country but have nothing to do with agriculture other than for a few garden products. Millions of families in the United States now live neither in city nor country and these constitute a new social class. They are neither peasants, proletariat nor capitalists, the three famous classes into which mankind was divided by Marx in the nineteenth century.

At the same time as the formation of this new social group there have been changes in the other classes and these likewise are of a revolutionary nature. The proletariat, or unskilled wage earner class, has very largely disappeared. The artisan or skilled worker has been replaced by a machine-tender in a factory. Instead of repairing things, we replace them. Capitalists as a class are changed. Instead of a few rich owners we now have millions of shareholders. Institutional buyers of market issues now replace the great money-men of the nineteenth century. Taxes cut deeply into the large fortunes.

This thesis of transformational change in the twentieth century could be expanded enormously but these illustrations suffice. However three other basic changes, completely revolutionary, should be marked out. These are instantaneous mass communication, the development of a non-Newtonian science and the reversal of long-term trends in family sociology.

BASIC REVOLUTIONARY CHANGES

Our century has witnessed the rise of instantaneous mass communication. The change is now so complete that with television one can communicate by emotion and communicate emotions. Nothing else in communication of feelings and emotions has been so drastic in its social consequences since the invention of

the community-wide Greek dramas of the city states in the fifth
century B. C. This social drama provided Aristophanes with a
medium whereby he could attack Socrates (*The Clouds,* 423
B.C but the trial and death of Socrates on the same charges
can only twenty-five years later. Now a single speech can change
the destiny of our one hundred eighty millions overnight.

The second of these basic revolutionary changes is the rise
relativity and the discovery of new worlds by our modern
sical science. We think of the discovery of the new world
the Americans by the Europeans in the sixteenth century as
ing a great addition. This was miniscule to the discovery of
e world of the atom during our century. The theory that worlds
xist underneath us is as old as Greek philosophy but the fact
hat we can penetrate therein with our minds and use this
knowledge is a product of the last few years. Now we know that
we live partly in a new non-Newtonian world, one of flux, creativity and atomic power. The last chapter of the last revision of
Einstein's work shows this difference in the puzzling new world.

The third great change, which is also entirely new, is the
rise of the family as a system of public social values. Never
before in history have a free urban and sophisticated people
made a positive change in the birth rate as have our American
people this generation. Prior to this time it was always the custom
for certain people to follow Malthusian tendencies and to breed
themselves into poverty or to control population by a high death
rate. These were the peasant and Asiatic peoples.

Westerners have always followed the traditional patterns of
race suicide. When they become urbane and sophisticated their
birth-rates fell and stayed below the reproductive rates. Each of
the great urban developments has seen the culture gradually
change from its former peoples into the hands of unsophisticated
"barbarians" who have not been able to carry on. In the past
generation this race suicide tendency of the west has been changed
in our culture. In 1860 there were about thirty-two millions of
peoples in the United States. Between 1935 and 1959 more than
fifty million Americans have been added by the birth-rate. This

is more than were here at the time of the Civil War of the last century.

We do not know what kind of a world we have changed into. But we do know that fundamentally a great chapter in history has ended and a new one has opened. What it means for us only time will tell but we know now that we really are in a new world. This is the nature of social change in our twentieth century.

THE MEANING OF THIS FOR THE FAMILY

Within this dynamic pattern we have the Western family and the American urban family system in particular. Fundamentally, modern family theory falls into three periods. The first may be called the nineteenth century doctrine, which covers the period from the French Revolution to the onset of World War I in 1914. The French Revolution seriously disturbed the family ideology of Europe both by experiments in France itself and by the spread of many new family ideas all over Europe through the Napoleonic law codes.

The second period of modern family sociology is equated with the extreme family reforms following World War I. These reforms differed in their extremity and perpetuation by country but fundamentally they were all alike in essentials—whether under Communism, Fascism or movements toward democratic totalitarianism.

The third period began at about the end of World War II and is still in existence. In essence it is a recovery or reaction to the social disorganization brought to a peak by the extreme family changes in the second period.

Nineteenth century sociology made "the family" a time-section in the picture of a constantly changing "domestic unit." According to all the popular theories of that century the nuclear family unit was a historical development and would pass away when the newer organization of society would be evolved.

In all of the major theories of society of the nineteenth century the family was included but increasingly, each step hypo-

thecated the domestic unit as becoming more and more a nominalistic, man-made, temporary, ever-changing-in-one-direction,
time-limited unit. This means that fundamentally family sociology
before World War I considered *the society of similar individuals*
as the only perpetual realism. The nuclear domestic family was
a dated creation. The family was considered to have a historical
beginning and eventually a similar temporal decay and replacement by some other domestic arrangement more adapted to the
modern mass world which was beginning to emerge.

The philosophical position of nineteenth century sociology
did not arise unexpectedly and out of the blue. It was an end
position, within the theory of limits, taking off from the complete
naturalism of society and all its major manifestations as codified
in the *Summa* of Thomas Aquinas. This work expressed the most
advanced social thought of the West toward the end of the thir-
teenth century. The steps toward the complete nominalist conception of the family were gradual but ever onward. By 1500 the
thinkers who were dominant in the academic realm of social
philosophy had yielded to nominalism in all areas except those
concerning the nature of the state and the family. The family
began to be considered very much nominalistic only after 1750.
The pure nominalist conception of the family became a cardinal
tenet of Marxist philosophy after 1850.

The great practical attempts at "factual" or nominalist organization of large segments of the Western family system came
in the decades between World Wars I and II. It was spearheaded
by legal measures against the family in Russia and in Germany
but was followed sympathetically in a psychological fashion in
certain other western countries, including ours.[2]

FAMILY SOCIOLOGY A GENERATION AGO

The main difference between the earlier position regarding the

---

[2] For this development see Carle C. Zimmerman, *Family and Civiliza-
tion,* Harper & Brothers, New York, 1947, Chapters 19-22; Otto von
Gierke, *Natural Law and the Theory of Society, 1500-1800*, (Tr. by Ernest
Barker), The University Press, Cambridge, England, 1934.

family in most nineteenth century sociology and the extreme views of the early twentieth century lay in the widespread later theory that the state had the "right" and the "duty" to extinguish the family as a "natural" social institution. The reason given for this need to break up the family as a legal group was to make the individual directly responsible to the political agency rather than as beforehand only indirectly through the family. Various phases of this philosophy appeared in many fields. In the United States it was widely held that the primary responsibility for the individual would change over to a new community form replacing the family. Social workers began to multiply in numbers and power and to deal more directly with the individual. This trend regarding the individual reached its high point at about the onset of the depression of the thirties after which it had to recede on account of the tremendous growth in the numbers needing help and supervision.

ATTEMPTS TO EXTINGUISH FAMILISM

With radical political measures, Russia in 1917, and Germany and Italy later began steady movements toward the new "right" and "duty." They attempted to extinguish the family by doing away with all older family law, except with retention of a slight deference to incest. This is what is called in legal terminology the rise of the "factual family" as opposed to the older "ethical family." [3]

The "factual" family is one that considers living together "marriage" and living apart "divorce." In such a social system, marriage and family have very few if any legal consequences. The Communists did it to get rid of the state (so they claimed) and the Fascists did it to make the state totalitarian (so they claimed). But both did it in a similar fashion.

In the United States during this period the conception of

---

[3] See the Association of American Law Schools, *Selected Essays on Family Law,* The Foundation Press, Brooklyn, 1950, all of Section 3, Part IV, especially pp. 907-937.

family responsibilities began to shrink. The change was achieved mostly by legal fictions, such as the widespread acceptance of separate jurisdictions for divorce alone—the rise of migratory divorce. The one and two child families began to be emphasized as most desirable. A philosophy of "eat, drink, and be merry" took over. "Puritanism" began to be called "a system of repressions." The idea of any individual restraint was considered as thwarting human life.

THE CLIMAX OF NOMINALIST FAMILY SOCIOLOGY

American fiction and drama began to desert the older theme of divorce as a *tragedy* and to present it as a necessary and even an *ennobling experience*.[4]

In the field of family sociology the older evolutionary teachings began to give away. The changes were manifested by the rise of the first books of a new kind of family sociology. This type is still popular, though changed considerably. It is called the "functional" approach. Probably the first of this new type of work appeared just five years after the last of the important older evolutionary and "improvement" texts, *Problems of the Family* by Willistine Goodsell, (1928).

The chief characteristic of this new kind of work is the inherent implication that the family is not a natural process of life but might well be made existentialist. It changes family teachings entirely from duty to choice. The implication is that all family life once started is easily escapable. Thus many do not see the role that the chain-of-being plays in the life of all of us.

A second phase of the change in family sociology during this period was the rise of the "functionless, affection only, school" of family sociology. Although preceded by a number of other studies, the work by William F. Ogburn in *Recent Social Trends*

---

[4] James Barnett, *Divorce and the American Divorce Novel, 1858-1937*, University of Pennsylvania Press, Philadelphia, 1939; D. N. Koster, *The Theme of Divorce in American Drama, 1871-1939*, University of Pennsylvania Press, Philadelphia, 1942.

in the United States, 1933, gave this ideology its great popularity in American sociology. In this development the Marxian version of the older nineteenth century school of social change is used as a plausible intellectual foil to misinterpret some meaningless statistics. According to this version, all functions of the family except affection, and possibly reproduction, have been taken over by other agencies. The weakness, invalidity and logical phantasy of these claims have been analyzed elsewhere.[5] Suffice it to say they gave one branch of the existentialist school of family sociology a plausible grounding in sociological theory and allowed the general philosophy of existentialism to take over.

The "functionless" and the "functional" schools of family sociology are sisters, in that one has to grow up to replace the other. Their children, from the philosophical point of view, have to take on a very moral "amoral" view of life as illustrated by Sartre, Simone de Beauvoir and the pleadings of the Kinsey reports.

CHANGES WITHIN THE FAMILY SYSTEM ITSELF

However, during the early twentieth century, commencing before 1920 and culminating in vaster developments after 1950, the family system of Europe and America began some changes of its own without regard to the directives, or their lack, furnished by the major family disciplines. These changes may be described as independent movements of the family systems, or key portions thereof, at self-discipline. The family made a gradual turn toward "natural unitism and realism." Secondly, since the change included only a portion of the families, and not all, some followed the older course and some the new. Thus a polarization of good and bad, or old and new family types began and has widened.

At first this polarization or separation of the older and newer family types was only minor and unnoticeable. Later about

---

[5] Zimmerman and Cervantes, *Marriage and the Family,* Henry Regnery Co., Chicago, 1956, pp. 64-91.

1950 it became violent. Thus it happened that after 1950 the Western world witnessed a most violent contrast of two family types, one semi-factual and one semi-ethical. For instance since 1950 in the United States we have seen the following contrasts.

THE ANTI-SOCIAL POLARIZATION

1. From the factual family system we have the highest level of real divorces (excluding immediate post-war fluctuations from hasty marriages) ever seen in Western society since such rates have been recorded. This rapid rise began among the civilian population sometime in 1942, thus violating and reversing the older alleged principle that wars and their resultant increases in social solidarity were associated with reduced divorce rates. After the war there were high peaks of divorces due to the re-turned soldiers, and then the situation settled down in its regular form with higher rates than before World War II.

2. From the factual family system we have also the highest rates for desertions and quasi-desertions of families that we have ever had. A quasi-desertion is an avoidance of the paying of alimony and support moneys legally due a deserted or divorced woman and her children. This is accomplished in the United States by rapid change of legal jurisdictions by the former husbands, so that the state and federal funds for aid to dependent women and children must provide the funds for support. The social work administrators claim the courts cannot keep up with the quasi-deserters. (In England and Wales alone these matters cost the public directly thirty millions of pounds in 1955.)

3. Also from the factual family system (assisted by war breakages) we have reaped a harvest of juvenile delinquency which is outstanding, and probably only equalled by conditions resulting from the Revolutions in France after 1798 (and its family demoralization) and that in Russia after 1917.

THE PRO-SOCIAL POLARIZATION

Contrasted with this, and on the good side, the family made

certain gains in the rise of the opposite group, the ethical system. This is measured by the following important facts:

1. For the first time in the history of a free, urban and rationalized family system, a vast and long-continued decline in the real birth rate is arrested, and a steadily increasing number of our families have moved from the one and two child types into the three-or-more child, or socially-reproductive types. This alone has junked all previous predictions as to the growth and size of the population of the United States of America.

2. This ethical family system has isolated itself from the "factual" families and surrounded itself with other good families of similar ethical views. Out of this pocketed situation it has been able to control its children to follow its views. By doing this it has been able to push the children upwards in the social system, so that now we have higher proportions of high school graduates and students in colleges and professional schools than any other time in our history. As a result the proportions of technically-trained persons in our social system is greater than at any previous point in history and the proportions of unskilled laborers in the country is now down near 10 per cent, the lowest proportion in history.

3. Finally, on the good side, is the fact that matching our high juvenile delinquency rates are the rates for unusually creative youth. More young persons now are doing more good and creative things than ever before in our history.

Thus the changes within the family system itself have been a movement toward a gradual reversal of the trend toward a nominalist and fragile, non-social, family type toward a stronger, socially creative unit. Some have continued the older way and others have moved progressively towards a newer adaptation. Such has been the general movement of the family not only in the United States of America but also in many important segments of the European community. We must now assay an explanation of this progressive movement and point out its influence on the subject of family sociology and research.

REVERSAL OF TREND IN THE FAMILY

Modern change in important phases of the American family system has been a subtle elusive thing and is as yet little understood. It had something to do with the environment of persons born between 1915 and 1920 and still continues. The mores of a culture move slowly like a giant pendulum but also very ponderously. For some generations up to the period of 1910-1915, the American birth rate moved slowly but surely lower. By the period 1910-1915, each "cohort" of 1000 American women were reaching new lows of reproduction. Then gradually after 1915, each 1000 female children born began to have at a given comparable age more children than the immediately preceding year's cohort.

As a result of the change in reproduction, all previous estimates of the size of the American population for the latter half of the twentieth century had to be revised radically upward. Between 1920 and 1940 the American population began to dip in the slant of its growth curve as if it were reaching a peak and would shortly stabilize or turn downward. The direction was reversed after 1940 as if it were moving toward newer and higher peaks.[6]

A second aspect of this trend toward family revival was marked by a conspicuous regrouping in the cities so that environmental control helped direct the motivation of the teen-agers toward creativity. In essence "good families" now surround themselves with similar families and the world of the child seems "good." That is what our study has demonstrated.

However, this is not the whole story. Conspicuous changes of a rational nature took place in such important European coun-

---

[6] Demographic figures are complicated and cannot be introduced here. Proofs of the above two paragraphs are given in W. S. and E. S. Wotinsky, *World Population and Production*, The Twentieth Century Fund, New York, 1953, pp. 44 ff.; *United Nations, Proceedings of the World Population Conference,* 1954, UNESCO, 1956, New York, Volume I, Meeting 6; P. K. Whelpton, *Cohort Fertility; Native White Women in the United States,* Princeton University Press, Princeton, 1954.

tries as Italy, France, Germany and Russia, not to mention others. In Italy the totalitarian movement toward "factual familism" inherent in Fascism, had to be given up early because of the great influence of the Catholic Church. However, that country is rapidly reducing its birth-rate to meet the challenge of over-population facing its culture and the movement is not directed by either a political power or a religion—that is, it is in the "private" mores.[7]

France, with a very low birth-rate for nearly a century, has reversed the trend during this same period. Germany, a country very completely dominated by the factual family ideology of Nazism, has shown a remarkable recovery toward ethical concepts.

The binding story, however, is in Russia which has not had a military defeat and has had the same political regime of Communism since 1917. By 1928 its family system as a legal and social arrangement had been almost completely shattered. The change towards ethical familism under the legal fiction of "for the good of the community" began in 1936. All factual aspects of the family system were completely abolished by the family laws of 1944. In all practical aspects divorce, abortion and the other evidences of the so-called "legal right and duty of family extinction" were then abolished. The new code was so rigid that it had to be corrected slightly toward more freedom in the legal changes of 1949.[8]

These are not all the changes nor do they refer to all countries, but they do include five of the more prominent and most populous countries of the West and concern families of more than a half billion persons in 1950. Nor were the changes all alike in the empirical sense. It showed as a decrease in the birth-rate in Italy, and an increase in France and our own. It showed similar changes in family attitudes in Russia with the same political

[7] See Carle C. Zimmerman, "American Roots in an Italian Village," *Genus,* Vol. XI, No. 1-4, Rome, 1955.

[8] See P. A. Sorokin, *The American Sex Revolution,* Boston, Porter Sargent, 1956, Chapter V; R. Schlesinger, *Changing Attitudes in Soviet Russia: The Family,* London, Routledge and K. Paul, 1949.

regime continuing, and in Germany with the changes of regimes. The point is that the changes only become important from the family point of view if we view them collectively as a renascence of family realism, or ethicalism, in relation to the cultures as opposed to the older trends toward factualism, nominalism and cultural irresponsibility.

RELATION TO THE PRESENT STUDY

It is our feeling that the study reported on here has measured a part of this reversal of trend within our family system. If this is so and our results are true, this is a very encouraging sign. It means that our families have found out how to meet the new world with a workable system. We can't afford to go on being ignorant because that is incompatible with the Atomic Age. On the other hand, we cannot afford the decadence of semi-sophistication. The new world needs a new person who is both learned and familistic. Russia discovered this the bloody way. We believe America has discovered this the peaceful and intellectual way.

NAME INDEX

Anderson, N., 40
Aquinas, T., 210
Aristophanes, 194, 208
Aristotle, 12, 163
Augustine, 194

Bacon, F., 163
Ball, E., 152, 156
Barker, E., 168, 210
Barnett, J., 212
Barron, M., 162
Basil, 194
Beauvoir, Simone de, 202, 213
Bossard, J., 152, 156, 162
Borderick, C., 27
Bunyan, J., 35
Burlingham, D., 13

Cervantes, L., 12, 13, 45, 54, 137, 175, 213
Comte, A., 201
Cooley, C., 189
Coon, C., 189

Dante, Alighieri, 201
Defoe, D., 35
Dekany, E., 162
De Wors, R., 31
Durkheim, E., 86, 166, 167, 168

Erasmus, D., 204

Feldmen, F., 75
Fillmore, M., 178
Fitzpatrick, E., 129
Frampton, M., 190
Frazier, E., 14

Freud, A., 13

Gini, C., 153
Ginsberg, M., 166, 168, 191
Ginzberg, E., 129
Glick, P., 30, 91, 103, 126
Glueck, E., 90
Glueck, S., 90
Goodsell, W., 212

Hanssen, G., 105
Hesiod, 163
Hobbes, T., 203
Hobhouse, L., 191
Homer, 70, 163

Jacobson, P., 47, 88
Jerome, 194

Kaster, P., 212
Kennedy, P., 162
Kinsey, A., 202, 213
Koos, L., 74
Kropotkin, P., 166, 168
Kulischer, E., 129

Landis, J., 162
Letts, H., 162
Le Play, F., 190, 199
Locke, H., 162
Locke, J., 203
Lucretius, 205

Machiavelli, N., 201
Malthus, R., 208
Marx, K., 168, 201, 204, 210, 213

219

TOPIC INDEX